CHATHAM HOUSE PAPERS

SOVIET POLICY PERSPECTIVES ON WESTERN EUROPE

T0346689

CHATHAM HOUSE PAPERS

General Series Editor: William Wallace
Soviet Foreign Policy Programme Director: Alex Pravda

The Royal Institute of International Affairs, at Chatham House in London, has provided an impartial forum for discussion and debate on current international issues for some 70 years. Its resident research fellows, specialized information resources, and range of publications, conferences, and meetings span the fields of international politics, economics, and security. The Institute is independent of government.

Chatham House Papers are short monographs on current policy problems which have been commissioned by the RIIA. In preparing the papers, authors are advised by a study group of experts convened by the RIIA, and publication of a paper indicates that the Institute regards it as an authoritative contribution to the public debate. The Institute does not, however, hold opinions of its own; the views expressed in this publication are the responsibility of the author.

CHATHAM HOUSE PAPERS

SOVIET POLICY PERSPECTIVES ON WESTERN EUROPE

Neil Malcolm

The Royal Institute of International Affairs

Routledge
London

First published 1989
by Routledge
2 Park Square, Milton Park, Abingdon, Oxon, OX14 4RN

Transferred to Digital Printing 2006

Reproduced from copy supplied by
Stephen Austin and Sons Ltd, Hertford.

British Library Cataloguing-in-Publication Data

Malcolm, Neil
    Soviet policy perspectives on Western
    Europe. — (Chatham House papers; ISSN 0143 — 5795)
    1. Western Europe. Foreign relations with
    Soviet Union   2. Soviet Union. Foreign
    relations with Western Europe
    I. Title   II. Royal Institute of
    International Affairs   III. Series
    327.4704

ISBN 0-415-03901-0

CONTENTS

PREFACE

This study assesses the rationale and prospects for the USSR's current European policy, taking into consideration patterns of thinking about foreign affairs among the community of expert advisers in Moscow. It is not assumed that there is a straightforward correspondence between the calculations of the Kremlin's policymakers and the contents of Soviet foreign affairs journals. Even less is it implied that civilian specialists have a dominant influence on policy, although they have recently been enjoying a period in the limelight. Nevertheless, Soviet expert writing on international affairs provides valuable insights in a field in which other kinds of evidence are in short supply.

The conclusion of the paper is that Gorbachev's policy towards Western Europe arises logically from the new overall Soviet perspective on international relations, which stresses bridge-building and interdependence, rather than conflict and defensive isolationism. It rests on a more multipolar vision of international relations, but also on an acceptance of the strength and durability of established ties in NATO and the European Community. The USSR is striving to construct a special relationship between the two halves of Europe, but it has no illusions that the deep-rooted special relationship between Western Europe and North America is about to crumble. In Moscow there is a new readiness to negotiate and a new realism about what can be accomplished. Thus there is a window of opportunity for the West, but many uncertainties remain to be resolved and obstacles overcome if a new European settlement is to be achieved.

I must thank all those who have helped in this project by reading drafts and offering suggestions for improvements, particularly Alex Pravda, for his encouragement and valuable advice; also Edwina Moreton, Margot Light, Jonathan Haslam, Roy Allison, Gennady Kolosov and other members of the Chatham House study group; and Hannes Adomeit and his colleagues at the Stiftung Wissenschaft und Politik in Ebenhausen. Although their efforts have helped me substantially in producing this study, I must of course bear full responsibility for any shortcomings.

I am also grateful to Pauline Wickham and her colleagues in the publications department at Chatham House, to fellow staff at Wolverhampton Polytechnic, and to my family, principally for their patience and forbearance.

The paper is published under the auspices of the Soviet foreign policy programme funded by the ESRC (grant no. E 00 22 2011).

March 1989   N.M.

1

INTRODUCTION

The rejuvenation of the USSR's foreign policy since 1985 poses a whole series of challenges to its international partners. Changes have occurred so rapidly and along so many different dimensions that it has become even more difficult than usual to interpret Soviet behaviour, or to form a conception of Moscow's underlying strategy. A special puzzle is posed by the Soviet Union's new European policy.

This aspect of policy has enjoyed maximum publicity right from the start of the new General Secretary's term in office. Indeed, even before his formal accession to power, Mikhail Gorbachev was talking of the need to protect the 'Common European Home' from the possible consequences of American plans for limited nuclear war. In one of his first statements on foreign affairs after gaining office, he remarked that although Soviet-American relations were 'an important factor in international affairs', 'we do not view the world solely through the prism of these relationships. We understand the importance of other countries.'[1] On his first visit to the West as General Secretary, in Paris in October 1985, Gorbachev offered direct nuclear arms reduction talks to the British and French, and held out the prospect of substantial cuts in Soviet intermediate-range missiles. Western Europe, he declared, was 'at the centre of attention in Soviet policy'. The Soviet Union was prepared to recognize and deal with the European Community as a political entity, and to work towards 'overcoming Europe's divisions into opposing groups in a more or less foreseeable future'.[2]

Introduction

In all this there was a substantial share of familiar Soviet 'open diplomacy', designed to put on pressure through public opinion rather than to lead directly to agreements. But practical proposals began to emerge, and by 1989 substantial progress had been made, or looked possible, in three areas in which negotiations had become hopelessly bogged down, or had been broken off, in the first half of the decade: intermediate-range nuclear missiles, conventional force reductions, and relations between the European Community and the Eastern-bloc Council for Mutual Economic Assistance (CMEA).

Arms control

Gorbachev maintains that the arms race is a primary cause of political tension, and not just an effect of it. He has therefore offered a series of concessions – recycling old Western proposals and sacrificing sacred cows of Soviet security-thinking – that are aimed at keeping up momentum in the direction of disarmament in Europe. The most spectacular result was the agreement signed in 1987 providing for the elimination of all land-based nuclear missiles with a range of 500–5000 km. By agreeing in September 1986 to disregard the plans of the French and British to modernize their strategic rocket forces, and by extending the deal in April 1987 to include shorter-range intermediate missiles (which represented a threat primarily to West Germany), the Soviet Union displayed sensitivity towards, and an unprecedented willingness to adjust to, the security interests of the major West European powers, and smoothed the way to removing one of the major irritants in international relations on the continent.

By coupling the talks with negotiations on space weapons and long-range rockets, Gorbachev pushed into the foreground the common interest of East and West Europeans in putting a brake on the Strategic Defence Initiative (SDI). This was a recurrent theme in diplomatic approaches to the United Kingdom, whose leaders the Soviet government has cultivated with special persistence. Although the British made no secret of their opposition in principle to Moscow's proposals to eliminate nuclear weapons in Europe, Gorbachev was unabashed. He made a point of interrupting his journey to Washington at the end of 1987 in order to hold talks with Margaret Thatcher, while TASS declared that relations between the two countries were better than at any time since 1945.[3]

In the field of conventional arms control, the Soviet Union promptly removed long-standing obstacles to progress by acknowledging substantial Warsaw Pact superiority in particular categories of weapons, and accepting intrusive verification procedures. The new attitude to verification was crucial in bringing to an unexpectedly successful conclusion the Stockholm talks on Confidence- and Security-building Measures and Disarmament in Europe in September 1986. *Pravda* declared that the 'new thinking' had taken root on European soil. Speaking at the United Nations in June 1988, Eduard Shevardnadze, the Soviet Foreign Minister, outlined plans for a three-stage disarmament process. In the first phase, NATO and the Warsaw Treaty Organization would exchange data and permit wide-ranging on-site inspection in order to identify and then remove conventional force asymmetries. In the second, each side would reduce its manpower by half a million. Finally, in the last phase, would come further troop cuts, accompanied by a transition to non-threatening, clearly defensive deployment patterns. A major campaign was soon under way to force progress in the talks on conventional forces in Europe (CFE) that were due to begin in 1989.[4] In December 1988 Gorbachev announced plans to cut Soviet forces by half a million men, to remove six of his thirty tank divisions in Eastern Europe and to withdraw an equal number in the western Soviet Union, along with sizeable quantities of artillery and combat aircraft. In January 1989 the Soviet Foreign Minister declared his country's intention of unilaterally destroying its stocks of chemical weapons. Shortly afterwards plans were made public in Moscow to withdraw certain short-range nuclear missiles from the European theatre.

Economic relations

Little progress was made at the talks held between the CMEA and the European Community from 1977 to 1981 because of fundamental differences of approach. Community negotiators were prepared to agree to mutual recognition and cooperation with the CMEA on such matters as forecasting, statistics and environmental protection. They insisted, however, that trade agreements must be negotiated directly between the Commission and individual East European states. The Soviet Union, on the other hand, wished to avoid a situation in which a united West European organization could dictate terms to small countries in the Eastern half of the continent, and wean them away from their bloc ties and obligations. It therefore demanded equal status for the CMEA and the EC.[5]

When the CMEA requested new talks in September 1985, however, it no longer proposed a (potentially restrictive) CMEA-EC trade agreement, but merely a 'joint declaration', which would 'create more favourable conditions for the development of relations between member countries of the CMEA separately and the EEC'.[6] The Commission pointedly accompanied its agreement to enter negotiations with the announcement that it had written to the individual CMEA member states inviting them to institute direct links with the Community. By May 1986, all without exception had responded positively.

Accord between the two associations was swiftly reached on the main points of an agreement during the period from March to May 1987 (described in Moscow as 'the year of Europe' in Soviet diplomacy).[7] The Soviet side showed unexpected flexibility in accepting references to West Berlin as part of the EC for purposes of the planned joint declaration. By the time the documents were signed the following summer, bilateral trade and cooperation deals were being constructed with Hungary (concluded in July 1988) and Czechoslovakia. Soviet officials made regular visits to Brussels with proposals for 'the widest possible cooperation'. A delegation from the Supreme Soviet visited the European Parliament in October 1987, official relations between the USSR and the European Community were established in August 1988, and in January 1989 the Soviet Foreign Minister attended formal talks with the Chairman of the EC Council of Ministers to discuss the 'framework and format of EEC-USSR political dialogue'.[8] It was made clear that the CMEA states were especially keen to participate in international science and technology programmes.

The Soviet leadership refused to be discouraged by the unforthcoming public response to its European diplomacy in London and Paris. In time, however, the focus of attention shifted towards West Germany. Here Moscow's persistence was in the end more obviously rewarded, as common interests in particular disarmament projects, and in trade and technology cooperation, began to take effect. Repeated calls to 'take Gorbachev at his word' began to emerge from the Foreign Ministry in Bonn. More evidence of the effectiveness of the new policy followed. In the spring of 1988 a proposal for a new 'Marshall Plan' for the economic reconstruction of Eastern

Europe was floated by the Italian industrialist Carlo de Benedetti, and swiftly endorsed by Giscard d'Estaing and by an editorial in *Le Monde*. The newspaper argued that such a project could 'élargir le poids de l'Europe dans le monde tout en allégeant le sort de toute une partie de la population'.[9] The Greek Foreign Minister declared in July that during his country's forthcoming presidency he foresaw the European Community playing a more active role, building on its agreement with the CMEA to achieve new levels of cooperation, and intensifying the dialogue on arms control and disarmament. Across Western Europe, public opinion surveys showed rising popularity for Gorbachev and declining belief in a Soviet threat.

The USSR strives to enlarge the forum of debate and negotiation on East-West relations and arms control, trying to establish a more important role for the CSCE countries as a whole. The stated aim is to encourage the development of a (pan-) 'European consciousness'. In the early part of 1988, particular efforts were made to set up fresh seedbeds of new thinking – round-tables, research groups, working parties – with participation from East and West. Contacts with communist and other opposition parties and with academic institutions were intended 'to draw into the process of preparing a draft of the "common European home" a maximum not only of government but also of other political and public forces'.[10]

'European' rhetoric was present in Soviet leadership statements before Gorbachev, but it is he who has been largely responsible for propagating the idea of a continent-wide European identity. This rests, according to his book *Perestroika* (1987), on 'the common heritage of the Renaissance and the Enlightenment, of the great philosophical and social teachings of the nineteenth and twentieth centuries', a heritage which carries with it 'a tremendous potential for a policy of peace and neighbourliness'.[11] The need for joint action is pressing, it argues. Europe faces threats of war, ecological catastrophe, irrevocable division into two political-economic integrated units, disaster in the Third World. At the same time it is well placed to pioneer inter-system cooperation, writes the General Secretary, because of its recent shared experience of war, its accumulated political skills, its scientific, technological and economic potential, and its existing network of contacts and agreements.[12]

The Soviet leaders frequently make the point that their European policy is not intended to exclude the United States. The Helsinki

5

process, in which the United States and Canada are full participants, is often put forward as a precedent and model.[13] Yet occasionally, especially in non-diplomatic forums, 'Europeanism' and 'Atlanticism' are flatly counterposed by Soviet spokesmen, in a way which seems to cast doubt on such assurances.[14] Soviet policy, indeed, has skilfully and publicly exploited transatlantic differences of opinion on East-West and West-South relations. The Political Report to the 27th Congress of the Soviet Communist Party in 1986 emphasized the waning of American hegemony and its political consequences:

> For the first time, governments of some West European
> countries, the social democrats and liberal parties, and the
> public at large have begun openly to discuss whether present
> US policy coincides with Western Europe's conceptions of its
> own security, and whether the United States is going too far in
> its claims to leadership.[15]

The rise to prominence in Moscow of Aleksandr Yakovlev, who has repeatedly expressed similar views about American relative decline and the prospects for West European self-assertion, and expressed them in a tone strikingly hostile to the United States, encouraged speculation that the new Soviet leadership was constructing its foreign policy on fairly radical assumptions about the speeding-up of trends to multipolarity in the West.[16] There is no doubt that a certain redirection of diplomatic effort has taken place towards Western Europe, and also towards Japan and some of the newly industrialized countries; but what does the Soviet Union hope to achieve as a result? In Pierre Hassner's words,

> Is Gorbachev's overture to Europe simply a tactical move
> meant to improve the Soviet negotiating position with regard to
> the United States, which would remain the main interlocutor?
> Or does the Soviet Union aim to replace the United States as
> the ... manager of the European security system?[17]

As another author expresses it, are plans being forwarded to break up the Western alliance and Finlandize Western Europe, or are we merely witnessing a more sophisticated attempt 'to unite Western policymakers behind certain policies favourable to the Soviet Union'?[18]

It is not an easy matter to find answers to questions of this kind. The material provided by Soviet diplomacy and propaganda offers rather slippery and unreliable evidence for deducing real plans and intentions. So also do the world-revolutionary perspectives set out in the classic statements of Marxism-Leninism, and their remnants in the kind of rhetoric which until recently was ceaselessly beamed at the Soviet public and at activists abroad. And there are so many unknowns involved that calculations founded on assumptions about socio-economic characteristics of the Soviet system cannot take us very far in determining the USSR's international goals. Finally, whereas in the West reasonably open debate on national policy in foreign affairs has long been regarded as legitimate, it is only just emerging in the Soviet Union.

What is available is the large body of writing produced by Soviet foreign affairs specialists. Several hundred experts are employed in Academy of Sciences institutes in Moscow whose principal task is to serve the requirements of foreign policy. They sit with officials on consultative committees and debate with them at conferences. Several research institute directors and their deputies act as public spokesmen on foreign affairs issues at home and abroad, and some have been observed to be in close touch with the topmost levels of the state and the Party. Several are Central Committee members, and one has even been promoted on to the Politburo. The Gorbachev leadership has adopted for its own use many of the ideas developed by specialists during the 1970s, and appears to allow them a degree of access to the public unprecedented in Soviet practice.

Whatever the eventual impact of their writings on policy, and it may in many cases be negligible, it has generally been safe to assume that Soviet specialist writers design their analyses in such a way as to fit into existing official frameworks of thought. They are cautious about introducing unfamiliar concepts, and hesitate to make radically new judgments unless they sense that they will fall on receptive ears. During the Khrushchev and Brezhnev eras, if there was a violent dispute at the specialist level, for instance, it could probably be taken to indicate disagreement at the policy-making level.[19]

The changes which have occurred in Soviet politics since 1984 have made interpretation easier in some ways and more difficult in others. Aesopian language and indirectly expressed debate are less common than before. Denunciations of previous Soviet propaganda 'stereotypes' have begun to appear, along with straightforward recommendations for changes in policy. Especially when authors hold official positions, or are close to particular members of the leadership, we can get a more reliable idea than before of what alternatives are being considered. On the other hand, the easing of controls on expression means that particular individual opinions and proposals may be just that, not necessarily Kremlinological evidence.

Approached with an awareness of such problems of interpretation, specialist writing, once the persisting inspirational or manipulatory elements have been filtered out, can provide valuable indirect indications of leadership perceptions, priorities and policy preoccupations. At a minimum, sustained changes in how Western Europe is described reflect, as in the past, shifts in what the leadership considers desirable that the public should think about the subject, and shifts in what specialists consider to be sufficiently consonant with top-level views to be worth committing to paper. At a maximum, expert contributions may, as their authors claim, represent genuine inputs to the policy process, whether they have a prompt or a long-delayed, cumulative impact. They afford an insight into prevailing ways of looking at the world and reveal what kinds of factors are regarded as important in policy advocacy. In this way they can help to verify the kind of hypotheses about the logic of the USSR's conduct which outside observers have traditionally made on the basis of more slender evidence.[20]

Most of the Soviet writing which is used in the following three chapters comes either from small-circulation books or from the specialized foreign affairs journals *Mirovaya ekonomika i mezhdunarodnye otnosheniya* (published by the Institute of the World Economy and International Relations – IMEMO), *SShA: ekonomika, politika, ideologiya* (published by the Institute for the Study of the United States and Canada) and *International Affairs* (published by the Foreign Ministry and the *Znanie* Society). It has not been subjected to exact quantitative analysis, but has been selectively presented in order to give a sense of the evolution of the consensus (or most widely shared) view on particular topics, of the boundaries of debate, of persistent lines of division of opinion, and of the presence of particularly vocal special interests.

Special attention has been paid to the work of individuals who operate at the frontiers of the specialist and the public world: institute directors and department heads, party and state officials with an academic background or research responsibilities, certain columnists in the central newspapers. They are more likely to reflect the attitudes of policy-makers than their less prominent colleagues, and perhaps to exert some influence on them. Those of them who hold academic posts are more likely to express any consensus view which emerges from the round-table meetings, conferences and working parties which they chair.

It might be objected that to focus on the output of civilian international affairs experts in research institutes and in the Foreign Ministry gives a partial impression of Soviet perceptions. More traditional views are undoubtedly prevalent in military and conservatively minded circles, although they have been given little expression in recent years. It is not the purpose of this study to provide a comprehensive survey, but rather to explain the ideas which at present dominate the scene and underpin Gorbachev's foreign policy. It is intended in this way to make clearer the rationale of that policy.

Soviet specialist writing has already been used to investigate changing perceptions of Western Europe. Hannes Adomeit, for example, detected four stages in the evolution of Soviet assessments. In the 1950s, he concluded, the EEC was seen as an American-sponsored project designed to weaken the position of socialism on the continent. In the 1960s its role as a weapon for defending West European interests against the United States came to be seen as more and more important, and optimistic judgments were passed about its future key role in world politics. In the second half of the 1970s, as the Community's economic problems deepened, Soviet commentators revised their views again and began to emphasize transatlantic interdependence. Autonomy from the United States was not developing as rapidly as expected. Finally, Adomeit tentatively identified the early 1980s as a period when Washington was seen to be engaged in a counter-offensive intended to reassert its dominance in the West.[21]

The aim here is to determine how this 'fourth period' in Soviet perceptions has developed. Has there been a revision of the 1970s image of interdependence and alliance unity? How do Soviet authors picture the balance of cooperation and competition inside the Atlantic partnership, and how do they assess the balance of power between its two components? What prospects do they see for Western Europe acquiring a political and military influence in the

world proportionate to its economic weight, and what do they see as
the likely consequences for East-West relations of greater West
European solidarity? What kind of fit is there between these
perceptions and Gorbachev's European strategy as it has been
pursued over the past four years? Are the concepts they have
generated and the policies they have informed adequate to the
realities of the 1990s?

It is argued that the new Soviet policy perspectives on Western
Europe can be understood only in the context of the overall new
thinking in foreign policy. Underlying Moscow's public recognition
of 'interdependence', and advocacy of cooperation and compromise
between East and West, is a radical shift away from zero-sum, *kto
kogo* conceptions of international affairs. This has affected interpret-
ations of West-West as well as of East-West relations.

Chapter 2 explores the roots of these new attitudes in the work of
Soviet foreign affairs specialists since 1945, and demonstrates how
Lenin's emphasis on the conflictual elements in relations between
capitalist states has tended to be replaced over the decades by an
emphasis on tendencies to cooperation. A 'global internationalist'
view of the world has emerged, which stresses the unity of the world
economy and the possibilities for international economic regulation.
In this perspective regional integration, such as in Western Europe,
appears as a step towards worldwide internationalization. A smaller
number of writers focus, by contrast, on tendencies to conflict
between regional 'power-centres' (in North America, Western
Europe, Japan).

In Chapter 3 it is shown how the new political climate in Moscow
has encouraged much more positive assessments of the process of
integration in the European Community, and much less disapprov-
ing accounts of its political implications, than in the 1970s. After a
fairly rapid evolution, the balance of published opinion now appears
to have shifted from a critical view which is close to the original line
held by the French Communist Party to a position – occasionally
even an enthusiastic one – which is closer to that of the Italian Party.
Writers in the 'power-centre' tradition are optimistic about the
prospects for Western Europe emerging as an entity able and willing
to defy Washington. The majority view, however, brings into the
foreground the continuing domination by the United States of the
Western political and economic system.

Changing Soviet conceptions of the international role of Western

Europe are discussed in Chapter 4. During the first Reagan administration most Soviet foreign affairs specialists gave the appearance of expecting that the European members of NATO would continue to show the increasing independent-mindedness which they had acquired since the 1950s and would strongly resist American attempts to put pressure on the USSR. This phase in perceptions came to an end in the mid-1980s, as the depth of alliance solidarity demonstrated itself. Western Europe was still described as a force for moderation, but as a rather weaker one than previously. A new frankness emerged in published work about the force of the 'Soviet threat' as a factor encouraging Atlanticist attitudes in the region. A third phase began after the Reykjavik summit in October 1986, when it began to be appreciated that countries such as France and the United Kingdom could play an important non-'constructive' role in East-West military relations. As *glasnost'* advanced, Soviet foreign affairs specialists were able to call publicly for the USSR to pay more attention in its diplomacy to West European security concerns. Another reason for moving towards greater 'Europeanism' in policy was seen in the benefits promised by the developing 'new era' in relations between Moscow and Bonn.

Chapter 5 examines policy towards Western Europe since 1985 in the light of what has been said about perceptions. In harmony with the specialist commentary of the period, which predominantly emphasizes the cohesiveness of the Atlantic community and of its West European component, the leadership has called for stability and continuity, and has expressed a desire to preserve existing alliance structures in the foreseeable future. It has various reasons for adhering to such a line, but a part has been played by changes in conceptions of international relations which mean that Western unity, whether on an Atlantic or a West European scale, must not necessarily be regarded as a bad thing from Moscow's point of view. Pressures are indeed applied to particular states, and leverage is exerted, but as part of an overall plan to reach agreements on the basis of mutual concessions (sometimes more on the Soviet side than on the West's).

During the 1980s, it is argued, the emphasis in Soviet diplomacy has remained essentially on relations with the United States, but it has shifted from time to time, giving more or less attention to one region or another. So far as East-West relations are concerned, such shifts appear to fit well with the three-stage evolution of perceptions outlined in Chapter 4. This means that more effort is currently being put into building links with Western Europe, with particular reference to West Germany. What is going on, however, is a readjustment of policy, not a fundamental shift. It is part of a general overhaul designed to make the USSR's international activities more effective by exploring possibilities in all parts of the world. The evidence of personnel changes suggests that a balance is being kept between Europeanist and Atlanticist tendencies in the Soviet foreign policy establishment, and that the options corresponding to different theoretical positions are being kept open.

The final part of the chapter considers various aspects of Soviet/West European relations. There is a discussion of the motives which may have induced Moscow to make such large concessions in the sphere of economic relations and CMEA-EC ties by comparison with the Brezhnev period, and of the logic which underlies the relaxation of controls on contacts between Eastern and Western Europe. Soviet actions appear to confirm conclusions reached earlier in the chapter about the present administration's preference for bridge-building rather than barrier-raising and wedge-driving. In regard to military relations on the continent, the forces pushing the USSR towards a radical disarming posture are reviewed. The course of Soviet/West German relations since 1984 is used to illustrate the way Moscow continues to manipulate differences of interest and perspective inside the Western alliance for its own ends.

The last chapter examines the uncertainties which surround the prospects of the Soviet project for a 'Common European Home'. It concludes that, whereas the general foreign policy line of the USSR is probably fairly stable, the Soviet conception of the future of Europe is by no means clear. The continuing debates described in earlier chapters are paralleled by ambivalence at the top level, especially concerning the relationship which it is envisaged the United States will enjoy with the Common Home. A second source of uncertainty is provided by political developments in Eastern Europe, where a loosening of Soviet-imposed discipline, combined with lack of clarity about the bounds of the permissible, could give rise to a whole range of outcomes, some extremely destabilizing in East-West relations. A third problem arises from the difficulties likely to be experienced by the Western alliance in devising and maintaining a coordinated response to Soviet initiatives.

It would be incorrect to suppose that the improvements in the quality of Soviet published analysis which have occurred gradually, over the last three decades, and rapidly, over the last three years, reflect principally a process of learning by the authors themselves. They have in many cases had more to do with changes in the status of specialists and changes in the boundaries of what it is permitted to express in public (and probably to some degree in private). In that sense they point to 'learning' by other parts of the foreign policy machine and by the Soviet system as a whole. The 'new' thinking, now that it has been endorsed at the leadership level, holds out the possibility of building a new kind of relationship between the Eastern and the Western halves of the European continent. But there is a daunting amount of learning still to be done, on both sides, if this possibility is to be turned into reality.

2

INTERNATIONALIZATION AND REGIONAL INTEGRATION

In international relations, wrote Lenin, 'two trends exist: one which makes an alliance of all imperialists inevitable; the other which places the imperialists in opposition to one another.' He pictured a shifting balance between cooperative ('centripetal') and conflictual ('centrifugal') tendencies.[1] According to Soviet doctrine, *both* these tendencies are intensifying. At the 27th Congress of the Communist Party in 1986, it was declared that 'capitalism now has to cope with an unprecedented interlacing and mutual exacerbation' of all its internal conflicts. There were 'new outbreaks of inter-imperialist contradictions' of an 'especially acute and bitter' kind, in particular between 'the three main centres of imperialism' – the USA, Western Europe and Japan. The Congress documents also stated, however, that the network of economic, strategic and other interests which tied the three centres together could 'hardly be expected to break up in the conditions which prevail in the present-day world'.[2]

Foreign affairs experts in the USSR are able to use the 'two-tendency' framework as a convenient vehicle for reproducing Western analyses of 'cooperation and conflict' in international relations (including the bet-hedging of their sources). Yet their work has specifically 'Soviet' characteristics, too. One is the emphasis which is put on technology as the driving force of social and economic change, and on the way in which greater industrial specialization has steadily internationalized economic life. The more innovative economists conclude that in consequence there has emerged a single, all-embracing 'world economy', in which the capitalist world economy and the socialist world economy are present as sub-systems.[3]

Internationalist images of the world economy were used for many years by Soviet social scientists as a weapon in their campaign against policies of economic autarky and political isolation. They were frequently encountered in the output of foreign policy research establishments, such as the Institute of the World Economy and International Relations (IMEMO). In the end they became the basis of a new academic orthodoxy.[4]

Another element of the Leninist legacy which Soviet foreign affairs specialists exploited for their own purposes was the idea of the strengthening of the state in capitalist (or rather 'state-monopoly capitalist') societies. Political scientists argued, for instance, that governments had achieved greater freedom of manoeuvre vis-à-vis business interests, and could pursue long-term goals of a rational kind, such as making agreements with the USSR. Economists, for their part, pointed to the extensive planning and coordinating powers acquired by governments. As early as 1946 it was being claimed that the capitalist system was not after all on the point of collapse: it had shown that it was able to adjust in a creative way to social change, to exercise some control over its economic processes and to maintain its technological vigour.[5] These views were energetically promoted by IMEMO scholars under Khrushchev and Brezhnev. The dignified explanation which they offered was that Western leaders had been forced to adapt in response to the changed balance of forces in the world, and in particular to the the growing power of socialism. However, the message which mattered was that a Soviet Union which cut itself off from the international division of labour would be not only forgoing the obvious benefits of specialization and economies of scale, but condemning itself to isolation from those societies which were likely to be leading the 'Scientific and Technological Revolution' for many years to come.[6]

The trend to cooperation

Most Soviet international affairs writers maintain that during the 1980s tendencies to regulation and coordination had the upper hand in the world economy. Technological change was accelerating, and the emerging areas – microprocessors, laser engineering, new materials, biotechnology – were so capital- and research-intensive that it was becoming more and more essential to specialize and to

15

plan production for a global market.[7] As a result, more determined attempts were being made, as they expressed it, to bridge the gap between the national scale of economic regulation and the international scale of capital flows and production. Already by the middle of the 1970s, wrote Anatoly Shapiro, a senior international economist at IMEMO, decision-makers in the West had become sufficiently conscious of the growing interdependence of their societies to set about establishing a new institutional framework for cooperation:

> How can we describe the international mechanism of state-monopoly regulation which is to replace the old system? It would be premature to announce that it has already been formed ... Nevertheless, one can say that the system of regulatory institutions is steadily being constructed, as a complex, multi-stage, multi-tiered mechanism operating on bilateral and multilateral, regional and international, inter-state and private-monopoly principles.[8]

Several of his fellow economists echoed Shapiro's view that the Western summits of seven, for example, are part of the emerging framework of an 'inter-state monopoly capitalism', which combines liberalization and a preference for indirect levers of economic regulation inside the separate national economies with a drive to coordinate policies more thoroughly at the international level.[9] Although they invariably draw attention to the destructive effects of elemental capitalist rivalry, Soviet writers sometimes seem, if anything, more willing to acknowledge that progress is being made in international economic management than their Western counterparts are.[10]

The place of regional economic integration
While a thoroughgoing globalist like Shapiro describes regional integration as an ineffective project, disruptive and counterproductive from the point of view of the world capitalist economy as a whole,[11] most writers see regional groupings as a component, a natural intermediate phase, in overall internationalization. Thus the West European grouping, in their view, will no doubt one day dissolve in a larger one, possibly on an Atlantic scale. Even now it enjoys only limited freedom of action. As one IMEMO economist

put it in 1978, 'Capitalism is faced with the need to regulate world-economic relations on a territorially wider scale than is possible within the limited regional framework of the West European integration machinery.'[12]

The most common way of talking about regional integration, then, is to treat it as a particularly intense form of internationalization. The growth of credit, trade, currency, production and other ties between states leads to the formation of a network, as one author expresses it, which is 'thicker' in some places than in others. In certain parts of the world it becomes so dense that the national economies which are caught up in it can no longer function independently of each other. As a result, governments are forced down the path of economic policy coordination, and 'regional integration complexes' are created. The boundaries of such complexes are not, however, clear-cut. Soviet writers note that the geographical spread of integration depends on which part of the economy is being looked at. It is typically narrower, for instance, in the sphere of manufacturing, and broader in the sphere of trade, while capital investment and currency operations are carried out on a transatlantic or even on a global scale.[13]

A third, and less thoroughgoing, internationalist perspective highlights centrifugal tendencies and inter-regional (especially European-American) rivalry.

Specialists who deviate from the consensus often have obvious political motives for doing so. In the IMEMO journal in 1988, for example, a Hungarian economist was criticized for arguing that regional economic integration was outdated (and by implication that the CMEA member states should orientate themselves more to Western markets). This is a doubtful thesis, argued the reviewer, declaring that integration on a *regional* basis was 'not only a consequence of economic internationalization but the highest form in which it is expressed at the present time'. The countries of Western Europe, she pointed out, had recently been forced to combine their forces more systematically in order to resist pressures from the United States.[14]

The 'West European power-centre' was generally considered by Soviet international affairs experts during the 1970s to have gained ground rapidly at the expense of the United States, but by the following decade the consensus view was that this readjustment had slowed down or gone into reverse. Several authors, however, stood out against this trend of opinion and continued to emphasize the

relative decline of American power, connecting it with an intensifica-
tion of conflicts inside the Western system.[15] Both in 1984, when he
was still Director of IMEMO, and in 1986, when he had not yet been
appointed to the Politburo but was already a senior Central Committee official, Aleksandr Yakovlev forcefully stated his conviction
that in the foreseeable future centrifugal tendencies would
predominate, bringing sharper conflicts and 'further disintegration
of the postwar monocentric capitalist world'.[16]

Yakovlev's writing has a strongly anti-American colouring. 'The
strategy and behaviour of the USA in its military, economic,
political and social-ideological components', he maintained in 1986,
for instance, 'has come more and more clearly into objective
contradiction with the interests of mankind as a whole.'[17] In his
version of events, the forces of American militarism and reaction
employ threats of coercion and the financial power of the transnational corporations to enforce their will on the other NATO states,
with the connivance of local 'Atlanticist' elites. The trend to
Europeanism among the allies of the United States appears as an
expression of mounting resistance to subordination, and it is associated with a more 'realistic', less military-oriented view of international relations.[18]

In the more orthodox, internationalist accounts, by contrast,
moves to greater interpenetration of the Western economies are
pictured as part of a progressive and dynamic process. They are seen
to be encouraged by, and in turn to stimulate, a sharper awareness
of interdependence. It is becoming more clearly understood, say
Soviet writers, that any ill-considered actions which seriously
infringe the interests of competitor states are likely to rebound
painfully on their initiators. In the political struggle between more
cosmopolitan groups associated with transnational capital on the
one hand, and groups associated with small and medium-sized
business on the other, the roles of hero and villain are reversed.
Protectionist attitudes, the IMEMO journal stated in 1988, are most
often 'associated with manifestations of chauvinism, with an inclina-
tion to use force to resolve international problems, to stick to a hard
line against partners and competitors, taking their interests into
account only minimally'.[19]

Conclusion
Internationalization has come to be treated by the majority of

academic foreign affairs experts in the Soviet Union as something which is both irresistible and beneficial.[20] The tendency to form regional integration groupings is perceived as part of, and as a step on the way towards, global integration. Internationalist habits of thought are particularly strong among the current generation of Soviet foreign policy specialists and advisers, and undoubtedly exercise at least a diffuse influence on the foreign policy establishment as a whole.

During the Stalin years it was predicted that the long struggle between centrifugal and centripetal forces in the capitalist world would eventually be resolved in the destruction of war and revolution. Now large-scale war is no longer regarded as probable, and increasing economic interdependence is considered to make even sharp political conflicts so destabilizing that they are likely to be avoided. It has even become permissible to speculate in the specialist press about the possible emergence of something resembling Kautsky's 'ultra-imperialism', or what the political commentator Aleksandr Bovin calls 'a transnational model of state-monopoly capitalism'. In such a climate of opinion, centrifugal phenomena were likely to be perceived as less important. They were likely to appear as short-term political and ideological counter-currents, overshadowed by the underlying trend towards greater consolidation.[21]

A small group of writers, including one influential official who is now a member of the Politburo, chose, however, to set the successes of regional consolidation in the context of global inter-regional conflict. In their view, regional power-centres were making a successful challenge to the dominance previously exercised by the United States and its transnational corporations. As might be imagined, this assumption generated a picture of relations inside the Atlantic alliance which differed markedly from the one painted by the internationalist majority.

3

WESTERN EUROPE: A NEW CENTRE OF POWER?

(a) The origins and motive forces of West European integration
The study of West European integration in the Soviet Union provides, in the words of one of its practitioners,

> One of the perhaps infrequent examples of how, despite certain well-known inhibiting factors, Soviet social scientists in the 1960s and 1970s continued to investigate international affairs in a creative way. The results of their work were reflected in the USSR's present-day European policy, in the idea of a 'European Home' and in the new approach to relations with the European Community.[1]

This happy state of affairs did not come about, however, without what the author calls 'a prolonged period of theoretical polemic'. IMEMO's 1957 'Theses' on the Common Market (and a second set published in 1962) comprehensively reflected the official hostility to the project. The first Soviet response to the EEC echoed Lenin's rejection of the slogan for a United States of Europe in 1917. Such an entity, he had declared, would be 'either impossible or reactionary', and could not last.[2] The Community was denounced as a probably short-lived attempt, sponsored by the Cold War planners in Washington, to mount coordinated resistance to the advances of socialism and national liberation. Soviet international affairs journalists predicted that it would encourage a swing to the right in domestic politics and facilitate German rearmament.[3]

This style of commentary is now far less common in specialist writing.[4] It was under attack, indeed, from the start. Even the 1957 statement acknowledged at one point that what was happening in Western Europe reflected the effects of a 'basically progressive' process, namely economic internationalization. As the years went by, IMEMO scholars amplified this idea, and developed the kind of theories of regional integration described in the preceding chapter.[5] Their case was restated in 1983 by Vladimir Baranovsky, now head of the institute's Centre for West European Studies:

> The thesis that there is an objective basis to West European integration, which is supported by the overwhelming majority of Marxist researchers, is of cardinal importance. It implies that the creation of the EEC cannot be treated simply as a consequence of political manipulation, or a fruit of imperialist policy. 'Integration appears', in the words of M. Maksimova, 'in response to the objective requirements of the forces of production. It follows from this that it would be utopian to think of preventing or halting it.'[6]

Economic and political factors in integration
While the economists were undermining the simple view of the EEC as an anti-working-class, anti-Soviet conspiracy by emphasizing its roots in 'progressive' economic changes, Soviet international affairs experts, starting in the 1970s, worked in the same direction by drawing attention to the growing independent-mindedness of the new 'power-centre' in its relations with the United States. Later, political scientists like Baranovsky began to criticize the 'automatism' implied in neo-functionalist and other economics-oriented explanations of West European integration. They argued that subjective factors – the convictions and political strategies of individual leaders like de Gaulle, for example, or the organizational interests of particular bureaucracies – could play a decisive role in events.[7]

A recent innovation in Soviet accounts has been to construct a renovated 'class analysis' of the development of the European Community, one designed to present integration processes in a progressive rather than a reactionary light. At the beginning of 1988

Yury Borko revealed to his Soviet readers that despite the opposition which communist parties put up to integration plans in the early years of the EEC, there was in fact widespread support for the project among the mass of the population. With the help of opinion-poll data, he argued that this support had continued to grow, contrary to the impression given 'in Soviet scholarly literature and especially in propaganda':

> On the one hand, the policy of integration is supported by the bourgeois parties, from the extreme right to the left radicals, by employers' associations, by militarist circles and so on. On the other hand, it is supported by the majority of organizations of the working class and the democratic intelligentsia, organizations which form the nucleus of the democratic camp in West European countries.[8]

It was neither anti-socialism nor economic factors which provided the initial driving force, in his version, but a widely shared vision of European unity as a guarantee against Franco-German conflict, as a means of increasing the region's independence and influence in world affairs, and as a way of preserving a common cultural heritage.[9]

Borko painted an encouraging picture of the prospects for change. He acknowledged the weakness of the socialist parties in Brussels, but saw grounds for hope in a new readiness on the left to cooperate and in signs of greater democratic influence on Community institutions. Among those signs were 'a noticeable widening of the scope of social policy', an activization of regional policy, the instituting of direct elections to the European Parliament and the extending of its powers. These last two steps, he argued, increased the Parliament's potential role 'as a democratic institution in Community decision-making'.[10]

(b) The consolidation of the West European centre

According to Hannes Adomeit, Soviet commentators in the 1970s tended to emphasize the failures of West European plans for integration. He summarized their view as follows:

> Economic integration at the macro-economic level has reached a threshold that the EC is unlikely to overcome . . . To a

considerable extent, therefore, foreign policy coordination and enlargement of the Community are escape mechanisms or ploys to convey the impression of forward movement where none exists.[11]

The balance of views has changed markedly since then. Soviet authors agree that there has been little progress in the direction of supranationalism, but they are on the whole generous in their assessment of what has been achieved on a predominantly *inter*national basis. Most appear to accept a broad definition of integration, which was first put forward in IMEMO in 1971, as a process that takes place in the framework both of 'European' unitary and inter-state agencies and of separate national agencies: it is seen not so much as a question of replacing existing institutions as one of encouraging them to interact more intensively and become 'Europeanized'.[12]

It is recognized that such a strategy has certain disadvantages: it is difficult to make radical changes in joint policy; member countries are likely to relapse into unilateral postures, which are promptly exploited by competitors like the United States.[13] Yet the picture which emerges in the work of a number of authoritative Soviet writers is of a flexible and adaptive system: 'a refined, technically well-equipped mechanism for inter-state manoeuvres to implement long-term political compromises'; the instrument for 'a new type of relationship between states, characterized by great stability and competitive collaboration'.[14]

The history of the European Community is portrayed by Baranovsky and his colleagues as a patient search for new institutional forms and new areas of activity, after an over-ambitious false start on supranational lines. In the 1960s, he writes, a customs union and the Common Agricultural Policy were successfully constructed, and organizational compromises were reached. In the 1970s the Community was expanded, and progress was made in foreign policy cooperation. In the 1980s further expansion has been accompanied by moves to achieve greater coordination of economic and especially monetary policy. This does not mean that a different strategy may not be chosen when the time is right. In the view of a number of writers the pragmatic character of the whole process, and the balance of 'federal' and 'confederal' forces inside the member states, mean that radical institutional change cannot be ruled out: 'The European Community retains a definite supranational potential.'[15]

The general tone of commentary on the preparation of the Single European Act (1985) and on the decisions associated with it was appreciative. One author declared that the signing marked 'an important milestone in the history of the European Community, capable of opening a new stage in the process of West European integration'. He suggested that the third (the political) stage of Walter Hallstein's European rocket was moving rapidly along its planned trajectory.[16] Like Yury Borko, some writers insisted on seeing far-reaching significance in the enlarging of the powers of the European Parliament.

In 1988 the Soviet press began to take more and more seriously the project to create a single, Community-wide market by 1992. There were signs that Moscow was beginning to share the apprehensions of other non-EC states that internal consolidation might raise barriers against the outside world. One specialist wrote:

> An expanded EEC market might make member countries less interested in East European markets ... Despite the current hardships in the the Soviet economy, contacts with the EEC market should be strengthened. We should work to firmly establish ourselves through trade, investments from West European countries in the USSR, and investments from Soviet enterprises in EEC countries.[17]

Some were concerned that old clichés about Western disunity were hampering Soviet efforts to adjust to the new realities. One Foreign Ministry official pleaded for more objective reporting:

> Recently newspaper headlines like 'The Common Market – Why the Deadlock?', 'Failed to Come to Terms', 'Differences Remain', 'Quagmire of Contradictions', 'Disunity of the "Common Market"' were quite common. And now in the EEC the tendency is to form one market: a powerful and effective mechanism of specialization and cooperation and a single currency system are being created, and programmes of fundamental and applied research are put forward. The EEC countries ever more often act in concord in international matters.[18]

Foreign policy
International rivalries of the kind which Lenin predicted would

doom any attempt at European union have received due attention in Soviet accounts of the EC. A particular focus of interest has been the pattern of disputes inside the Bonn-Paris-London triangle over issues such as supranationalism or greater European coordination in defence matters.[19] But these were not regarded as disabling. During the 1970s Soviet specialists noted that the Community member states were beginning to pursue a coordinated policy on international issues outside the narrow trade and tariff area (for example in the Middle East and in the Helsinki talks). In 1978 Mel'nikov wrote that the preceding decade had seen 'the gradual transformation of Western Europe into a special centre in the system of international relations', turning it from an economic into a political competitor of the United States. This impression was subsequently reinforced by more or less united action connected with the Soviet intervention in Afghanistan, the American-Iranian crisis, the Polish coup in 1981, the Falklands war and the dispute over the USSR/Western Europe gas pipeline. 'A new West European consciousness is emerging,' wrote Yury Davydov in 1986.[20]

Soviet authors warned that there was a long way to go before it would be possible to speak of a unitary West European foreign policy. Baranovsky insisted, for example, that the Community was far from emerging as a superpower: joint positions were being achieved only on isolated issues, and then only after a long and painful process of negotiation.[21] Nevertheless, by the 1980s Western Europe was beginning to be perceived as an important actor in world affairs in its own right. A leading Soviet theorist of international relations described it in 1987 as 'a political union of states', whose initial limited goal of encouraging regional economic integration had been superseded by the aim of 'widening and deepening its political tasks and functions, to the extent of working out a coordinated foreign policy with regard to particular international issues'.[22]

Industrial policy

There was less agreement when it came to evaluating the success of the Community's economic policies. Some considered that the drive to integration had acquired a new dynamism by the mid-1980s: long-standing disputes had been settled, or at least damped down (over the Common Agricultural Policy, UK budget contributions, research and social programmes); by setting up the European

Monetary System, a significant step had been taken towards creating a currency bloc; and plans had been laid for a substantial technological renewal.[23] A coordinated economic policy on monetarist lines had been conceived and successfully put into practice, reducing the rate of inflation and the share of government spending in the economy.[24]

Soviet writers maintain that a crucial role in relations between the advanced states is played by competition in science and technology – 'the nerve of inter-imperialist rivalry'.[25] West European attempts to build a technological community have accordingly attracted increasing attention. A round-table conference on the topic was organized at IMEMO in 1987. A number of those who attended painted an impressive picture of the progress which was being made. They pointed to the large number of joint research-and-development projects which had been started, to the careful selecting of priority areas, and to the way scarce resources had been used effectively by concentrating on pump-priming and coordinating rather than on direct financing.[26]

This was probably a way of proposing an alternative model for industrial and technological cooperation in Eastern Europe, where the methods used so far have on the whole been sadly ineffective. Those specialists who looked at West European integration programmes in the wider Western context, by contrast, drew less encouraging conclusions. They stressed global-internationalizing counter-tendencies[27] and European weaknesses. At the 1987 conference a number of the participants drew attention to the way American and Japanese banks had established a dominating presence in West European markets. Industry was perceived to be subject to strong pressures from outside: European firms were more likely to merge with, or invest in, partners outside the region than in each other. One speaker even proposed that what was going on was 'a process of erosion of the nucleus of monopoly capital in the region'. As the conference report expressed it,

> Despite the marked speeding-up of capital centralization in the region, the creation of 'European' companies had not become a mass phenomenon. The gap between Western Europe and the USA in the number, size and competitiveness of leading industrial companies had been closed only in the primary and other traditional sectors. In the most modern science-intensive

sectors the lag behind American and Japanese competitors had increased.[28]

For a convinced supranationalist like Yury Shishkov, the scholar who pioneered the Soviet study of economic integration in Western Europe, the failures of industrial policy reflect underlying political weaknesses. The Community, in his view, has proceeded by avoiding difficult choices, forwarding a freer market but leaving the main levers of economic regulation in the hands of member states. The active industrial policy which is urgently required in order to reverse the drift into technological dependence on the USA and Japan shows no sign of emerging. 'Stagnant' organizational structures, conceived of in the 1960s as a short-lived compromise solution on the path to an 'objectively necessary' federalism, have become an entrenched obstacle to progress.[29]

This kind of analysis is surprisingly rare in Soviet commentary, however. Discussion tends to focus on practical matters of the kind which have immediate implications for the USSR. Thus, in the late 1980s, particular attention was devoted to the Eureka programme. At the beginning of 1988 the then head of IMEMO's Centre for West European Studies launched a discussion of the project by posing three questions:

(1) Is Eureka a West European response to the US technological challenge, or merely an appendage of SDI?
(2) How committed to Eureka are particular states, corporations and the European Commission?
(3) What are the prospects for scientific and technological cooperation between the West and East European countries on the basis of Eureka and the CMEA's Comprehensive Programme for Progress in Science and Technology?[30]

Those taking part gave varied and contradictory answers. The Strategic Defence Initiative was often described by Soviet writers as a means used by the United States to demobilize European attempts to catch up in leading-edge technologies. The Eureka plan was accordingly welcomed as a sign of determination to cooperate in resisting this kind of pressure, with the long-term goal of creating conditions for greater political autonomy. As one enthusiastic specialist put it: 'The participating countries intend to make of

27

Eureka one of the most powerful weapons in their struggle with the USA and Japan for technological leadership. The project is seen as the first step on the path to technological unity in Western Europe.'[31]

Other participants emphasized the non-bureaucratic virtues of the project. Eureka had already reached the stage, it was claimed, at which it could do without further public funding and operate on a self-sustaining, decentralized basis. The project's 'bottom-up' principle of operation was described by one speaker as more flexible and more appropriate to 'the current stage of scientific and technological progress' than the centrally funded EC programmes (and, implicitly, the cumbersome CMEA ones). Several speakers painted a bright picture of Eureka's achievements so far, claiming that it was already encouraging many large firms to find local partners rather than American or Japanese ones.[32]

The predominant view, however, was that the United States had successfully manipulated the levers afforded it by its existing technological lead and its position in the alliance to avert any danger of a serious, concerted West European response to the challenge of SDI. The United Kingdom and the Federal Republic of Germany, it was noted, were swiftly enrolled as junior partners in the American project, and began to push for a compromise solution which would have the effect of reducing top-down funding for Eureka and making it supplementary to SDI rather than competitive with it. Unity had been undermined yet again by technological nationalism and by the 'Atlanticism' of the British and West German establishments.[33]

The question about the likelihood of East-West European cooperation on the basis of Eureka drew a more uniform but rather tentative response. An IMEMO survey at the end of 1987 had already summarized the views of West European socialists and social democrats concerning pan-European economic cooperation. It revealed some support for allowing CMEA member states to participate in Eureka projects. The (predominantly conservative) governments, it was noted, did not object to this, but opposed the idea of states being involved, and recommended that agreements should be signed by individual enterprises.[34] In view of the USSR's recent foreign trade reforms, and in particular the opening-up of possibilities for joint ventures on Soviet territory, the most promising route forward, they suggested, might be to adjust to the terms being offered, and to try to establish contacts at the level of research establishments and firms.[35]

(c) Towards an independent centre of power?

In the shifting inter-regional 'balance of forces', how do Soviet authors currently estimate the relative weight of Western Europe and the United States? Clearly, economic integration and political coherence are an important part of the arithmetic, but they may have little impact on their own. During the 1980s Soviet foreign affairs writers acknowledged that progress had been made towards closer coordination in foreign affairs, in the currency markets, in science policy. As we shall see in Chapter 4, they also commented on trends to increasing military cooperation. However, in the defence sphere, for instance, no one claimed that moves towards coopera-tion had substantially altered Western Europe's previous extreme dependence on the United States. Even Yury Shishkov, a writer who was not given to minimizing conflicts inside the alliance, acknow-ledged that the United States had as a rule *supported* the process of West European economic, political and military integration, on the assumption that it would serve mainly to consolidate the unity of the West as a whole.[36]

Any predictions which Soviet specialists might wish to make concerning the future correlation of power in the West and its effect on East-West relations must therefore be backed up by two further calculations:

(1) an assessment of the potential of Western Europe to become sufficiently strong – economically, militarily, technologically – to be able to assert itself in relation to the other 'power-centres';
(2) an assessment of political trends in the region. Is it likely to want to take a much more independent line, or is the prevailing Atlanticist tendency too deeply rooted?

Soviet attempts to cope with the second of these tasks will be discussed in the next chapter. The remainder of the present one reviews Soviet conceptions of Western Europe's capabilities.

Because the balance of forces is such a complex and indeterminate thing in Soviet usage, there is great scope for selectivity and tendentiousness in writing about it. Thus, while most authors followed the Western consensus view in the mid-1980s and took a cautious view of the future of the West European 'power-centre', a voluble minority, mainly Party officials, took up what might be called a 'strong Europeanist' position and refused to abandon earlier optimistic assessments of the region's prospects. We shall consider first of all the mainstream academic analyses.

According to Bunkina's *USA versus Western Europe*, first published in Russian in 1976, a serious weakening of America's postwar hegemony had taken place by then, particularly in the economic sphere. Shishkov likewise wrote in 1979 that the imperialist camp had been 'transformed from a single-polar to a multi-polar system'. Western Europe had emerged as a force in world politics and the pattern of forces inside the Atlantic alliance had undergone a significant adjustment.[37]

Even then, however, Bunkina warned that the recent relatively rapid changes probably represented a short-term trend: 'There is no reason for extrapolating this tendency into the future. Events have shown that in many spheres of the inter-imperialist struggle, American imperialism is fully capable of counter-attacking, holding and regaining its supremacy.'[38] The United States, various authors pointed out in the 1970s, dominated the NATO alliance militarily and politically. The dollar was a world currency. American transnational corporations were more numerous, more well-established and on the whole more technologically advanced than their European competitors.[39]

By the middle of the following decade, when the predicted counter-attack had taken place, most Soviet specialists were ready to acknowledge the upsurge in economic growth which had occurred in the United States and the strengthening of its lead in industrial investment, research and development. 'The industrial, scientific and technological potential of the USA is still beyond comparison with that of its principal competitors,' announced the IMEMO journal in 1986. 'The latter have failed to carve out a clear leading position in a single one of the key new areas.'[40]

Despite the successes which some analysts reported in its joint research-and-development activities, Western Europe, was most frequently pictured as coming a poor third in the high-technology race.[41] The United States, it was said, had successfully deployed its world-financial, technological and military advantages and had outmanoevred its rivals.[42] There was also a cool appraisal of

Western Europe's own handicaps – fragmented leadership, under-investment, structural problems – and doubts were voiced (see the preceding section) about its ability to push through the necessary restructuring in the face of transatlantic pressures and temptations.[43] Even those who warned that 'Europessimism' had been overdone were cautious about predicting a rapid reversal of the downward trend.[44]

In the midst of all this reappraisal the 'strong Europeanists' persisted in emphasizing the long-term decline in American relative power. They did their best to present Western Europe's current situation in the best possible light. Anatoly Kovalev, one of the two First Deputy Foreign Ministers and a veteran of his country's European diplomacy, the man principally responsible for the Soviet side in the Helsinki negotiations, wrote, for example, in 1986:

The potential of this region can be clearly seen from its share in the developed capitalist countries' industrial output, which has never gone below the 40 per cent mark over the past few decades, and its economic growth rate is on the same level as that of the USA. The West European countries have practically caught up with the United States as to the amount of foreign investment, and are even pressing the USA on its domestic market, selling to the US consumer their cars, ferrous metal-lurgy goods, footwear, textiles, and some other goods and services. The West Europeans go out of their way to prevent the USA and Japan from outstripping them in computer sciences, nuclear power engineering and outer space exploration.[45]

Aleksandr Yakovlev, whose 'centrifugal' conception of international economic relations has already been noted, described on several occasions in 1985 and 1986 how the United States was forced to respond to the mounting economic challenge presented by its European and Japanese rivals by resorting more and more frequently to military arm-twisting, exploitation of its financial position and straightforward protectionism. In the long run, he claimed, it would have to adjust to the loss of its leadership role, as the OECD, the Hudson Institute and various other organizations predicted.[46]

In 1988 Vadim Zagladin, deputy head of the Party's International Department, pointed to what he called 'a fermentation of ideas and thoughts' in Western Europe. The new science and technology programmes, he claimed, had 'achieved a great deal': 'Europe is rapidly becoming an increasingly serious economic, scientific and technological giant – mainly the FRG, and Italy, is making its presence felt, as well as others. This is already beginning to change the correlation of forces with other centres of power in the capitalist world.'[47]

The kind of individuals who embrace 'strong Europeanism', and the way they tend to disregard trends of opinion in the academic foreign affairs community, make it likely that changes in the frequency and intensity of that tendency in Soviet writing are determined overwhelmingly by political influences, either in internal Soviet or in international affairs. Some light will be shed on this political context in the pages that follow.

(d) Summary

The material which has been reviewed so far reflects processes going on at three levels. The first level is that of specialist argument and debate, such as might be encountered anywhere in the world, about the achievements and the prospects of West European integration (for example, about the interaction of economic and political factors, the likely future role of supranational elements, and so on). At the next level we can observe how the academic community as a body registers and evaluates new developments in European construction (for example, advances in coordination of foreign policy, preparing the way for a single market). Finally, there are the effects of changes in leadership attitudes. In recent years one such effect has been that the predominantly internationalist and Westernist specialist world has enjoyed greater freedom to discard traditional 'class-struggle' stereotypes and to write in more positive terms about developments in Western Europe. Another effect has been to encourage further politicization and to shape new patterns of debate.

At least until recently, those Soviet authors who chose to write about the progress of West European integration were choosing to stand out against the trend of official policy, which was to belittle the successes of the European Community and deny it recognition. One of them (see the opening paragraph of this chapter) has even claimed for himself and his fellow specialists a substantial part of the credit for reversing this policy in the mid-1980s. It is therefore appropriate to describe them all in general terms as 'Europeanists'. However, the recent greater freedom of expression has reinforced the impression that certain groups of writers have been exploiting the opportunity to write about Western Europe in order to make quite specific political points.

The most obvious message of their work was a straightforward internationalist one. They were trying to dispel the wishful illusion that the USSR and its partners could prosper and compete with the West in relative isolation. A second message was that, even in conditions of a severe deterioration in Soviet-American relations, detente could be preserved and extended by concentrating on other partners. These views were probably more or less universally held among civilian specialists. In the third place, attention was being drawn to the evidence that regional economic integration on market principles works, and – by implication – that the CMEA countries should learn from the West European example, and perhaps seek to be more closely associated with it.

A fourth point was connected with the prominent role played by social-democratic parties and policies in the life of the Community states: the USSR, it was being suggested, should abandon Bolshevik exclusiveness and exploit the common ground between the two socialist traditions. As time passed, it became increasingly clear that certain writers were campaigning to accelerate the rapprochement which was being fostered under Gorbachev between the CPSU and Western 'reformist' parties. Commenting on proposals from German members of the European Parliament that East European countries should be allowed to participate in the Eureka research programme, one writer declared: 'Now the time is ripe for activizing dialogue between communists and social democrats on this subject, focusing on the search for new effective forms of business exchange and cooperation.'[48]

This 'anti-sectarian' position overlaps with, but should not be confused with, the essentially anti-American 'strong Europeanism' expressed in the past by individuals like Aleksandr Yakovlev, which bases itself on the regionalist perspective described in Chapter 2. This standpoint is associated with a determinedly optimistic view of European construction, in which longer-term trends to multipolarity in the Western world are stressed and evidence of shorter-term problems is neglected. It implies that Soviet policy has lagged behind a substantial shift in relative power from America to Europe, and that greater reliance should be placed on left-wing, neo-Gaullist and pacificist elements in West European politics.

The 'moderate Europeanism' which predominates among specialists, by contrast, has its roots in the internationalist view of regional integration as part of a wider global process. It paints a much more dynamic picture of West European integration than Soviet writers did in the 1970s. Authors cite achievements in foreign policy coordination, enlargement of the Community, exchange-rate control, and research-and-development planning. Some even hold out the prospect of an evolution towards federalism in the foreseeable future. This is balanced, however, by a sober appreciation of failures, rather in the style of (sympathetic) Western observers. The prospects for technology and industrial policy in Western Europe and the region's future ability to compete with the United States and Japan are subjects of constant discussion and of fairly evenly balanced argument between Soviet Europessimists and optimists.

Western Europe has thus won acceptance as a coherent economic and political entity. Only a few Soviet authors, however, are ready to claim that the region possesses the kind of economic and political resources which would give it the capacity to assert a significantly greater degree of autonomy in the Western alliance. There is also some doubt concerning the will of Western Europe to make a bid for greater independence and the likely repercussions which such a move would have on East-West relations. Soviet writing on that topic is the subject of the next chapter.

4
WESTERN EUROPE IN
EAST-WEST RELATIONS

According to Soviet textbooks, the international actions of regional groupings such as the one centred on the European Community are motivated by a combination of *general* class interests, which dictate opposition to socialist and national liberation movements; *regional* monopoly-capital interests, in competition, for instance, with the United States and Japan; and *national* monopoly-capital interests. In the 1950s and 1960s, Soviet hostility to European integration was based on the idea that it predominantly served general class interests. The EEC was initially described as American-sponsored and anti-socialist in conception. During the late 1960s and early 1970s, as the West European countries began to pursue more independent foreign policies, Soviet commentators placed more and more emphasis on the second category of interests, and on inter-regional rivalry. Although subsequent events caused a certain swing back to the focus on transatlantic solidarity, and although national concerns are still seen as crucial, the emphasis on regional interests has remained. It represents a durable and substantial innovation in Soviet writing about international relations.[1]

West European interests in detente
During the first half of the 1980s, when the Soviet Union was relying on Western Europe to exert a moderating influence on American policy, specialists devoted a substantial amount of attention to specifying the political, economic and cultural factors which made the West European powers more attached to detente than the

United States was. Their conclusions resemble those to be found in Western literature:

> Because of their different experiences during the twentieth century and because of geography, Europeans and Americans had contrasting perceptions of war. The latter cherished an unrealistic sense of invulnerability which could lead to adventurism.[2]

> Western Europe had derived large, tangible benefits in the economic and security fields from detente in the early 1970s. Unlike the United States, it had a great deal to lose from a worsening of relations.[3]

> In the arithmetic of inter-imperialist rivalry, Western Europe's strengths were in the economic area. In the political, and still more in the military, sphere it was relatively weak. Thus Yury Davydov, the head of the US/West European Relations Sector at the United States Institute, wrote: 'Detente moves into the foreground the "power" of Western Europe, and moves its weaknesses into the background, making possible a better balance in its relations with Washington, and seriously hampering attempts by the United States to use its position as leader of the Atlantic alliance in order to exploit its partners economically, financially and politically.'[4]

> Relaxation of tension had enabled West European leaders, from de Gaulle to Kohl, to put pressure on Washington and influence alliance policy, by moving closer to Moscow on particular issues.[5]

> Differences in internal politics were also seen to be important. The USA's 'military-industrial complex' was judged to wield far greater political influence than its smaller and fragmented transatlantic counterparts. Whereas the West European left was an important factor in the politics of the region and had consistently been at least less hostile to the USSR than the right, there was no comparable force in American politics, and hostility to the Soviet system was widespread in all sections of society.[6]

Soviet authors used the terms 'Europeanism' and 'Atlanticism' to describe currents of thought in Western Europe that were more or less inclined to favour relaxation of relations on the continent and/ or a loosening of alliance ties. Initially Europeanism was associated by them with Gaullism, later with German SPD thinking under Brandt's leadership, and in the 1970s with independent aspects of European Community policy in international affairs. It was perceived as having diverse socio-political roots – 'technocratic', social-democratic and nationalist.[7]

Some comments about the potential of Europeanism have been enthusiastic. One specialist wrote in 1988 that the high point of detente in the 1970s had brought about, albeit temporarily, 'a radical shift in the balance in favour of those who support combining European integration with all-European cooperation', by drawing in on the detente side 'realistically thinking circles of a bourgeois-centrist and even conservative orientation'.[8]

By this time, however, such commentary stood out as optimistic policy advocacy, in the context of a wider discussion in which the dominant tendency was to downgrade assessments of Western Europe as a force for detente. The intervening years had obliged Soviet writers to revise their assumptions about what the West Europeans took their interests to be, and about their capacity to defend them. The three sections of the present chapter outline the successive stages of this reappraisal.

(a) Western Europe as a force for detente

Atlantic relations in the New Cold War
France's departure from the NATO unified command in 1966, West Germany's Ostpolitik, dissent by West European states from American policy in Vietnam and in the Middle East in 1973, and their energetic participation in the Helsinki process and in East-West European trade and cooperation all constituted chapters in what Soviet commentators of the late 1970s pictured as a process of intensifying discord inside the Atlantic community.[9] Observing Washington's attempts during the early years of the following decade to adjust to new circumstances and to control these conflicts, one writer concluded that detente and the continued existence of NATO were simply incompatible, and that the United States was ultimately obliged to set about destroying detente in order to preserve its leadership position in the alliance.[10] As the first Reagan

administration progressed, many appeared to accept that, even if it was not inevitable, this was indeed the strategy which had been chosen.

This is not to say that Soviet authors analysed Atlantic relations purely in terms of disagreements over East-West issues. As the last chapter has indicated, Reagan's 'global unilateralism' was most often interpreted as a way of striking at the USSR, at troublesome elements in the developing world and at his allies simultaneously.[11] In this view, the New Cold War served to strengthen bloc discipline and to reinforce waning Atlanticist sentiment. It enabled the United States to capitalize on its (military) strengths in relation to those of its partners. It also yielded benefits in economic competition: forcing the pace of military-technological advance and curtailing East-West ties worked to the detriment of nations with less arms-oriented and more trade-dependent economies.[12]

During the first Reagan administration, Soviet commentators noted that the allies seemed ready to put up strong resistance to American policy in areas which immediately threatened their security and economic interests. They may have been prepared to join in public denunciation of events in Afghanistan and Poland, but they opposed any serious retrenchment of detente in Europe. Washington's partners were praised for the independent-mindedness they had demonstrated at the Helsinki follow-up meetings, carving out a position quite distinct from that of the United States. Frequently commented on was the 'unprecedented diplomatic action' which they took by refusing to accept a ban on supplies for the Soviet-European gas pipeline in 1982. All in all, Western Europe's low-profile strategy of maintaining outward compliance but carefully distancing itself from the administration's position, backed up by consistent attempts to maintain European unanimity, was considered to have enabled the allies to preserve in relatively good order their links with Eastern Europe, and with Arab and other Third World partners. In one writer's opinion, the USA's attempts to disrupt Western Europe's relations with the Eastern bloc had met with such limited success that by the middle of the 1980s American leaders were being forced to review their whole policy strategy.[13]

A military power-centre?

For some authors, the tendency to greater West European autonomy in the alliance appeared to be spreading into the military sphere. At the end of the 1970s Soviet commentary about the prospects for European defence cooperation had been sceptical. By 1983, however, in his book *Power Centres*, Vladimir Lukin was declaring that although military integration still lagged far behind economic and political integration, in the new decade it had emerged from the embryo stage, and had become a matter for uninhibited discussion at the highest level. He pictured this development as the latest step in a chain of events initiated by France's withdrawal from the NATO integrated command in 1966. Thinking (aloud) about the 'unthinkable' option of breaking free from strategic dependence on the United States had over the years been 'a most effective instrument of pressure on the senior partner', he wrote. Recently doubts about the reliability of the US nuclear guarantee, about the strength of American conventional forces, and about plans for limiting nuclear exchanges to the European continent had put military-strategic issues firmly on the integration agenda. 'What is going on now', wrote Lukin, 'is a gradual but quite definite catching-up by the "European rear" with the position and the assessments associated with the Gaullist vanguard in the 1960s.'[14]

In this perspective, which was shared by certain other authors at the time, 'Europeanist' defence thinking expresses a striving for political autonomy by leaderships who sense 'the incompatibility of US foreign policy with their own countries' national interests', for example in detente and the avoidance of war. Their immediate goal was considered to be to achieve a more equal balance of influence on alliance decisions. Its Gaullist origins also implied a distancing from the traditional fixation on the Soviet threat as the focus of defence thinking.[15] In 1984 Gennady Kolosov concluded his book about British involvement in West European military cooperation by stating that although the political consequences of this process were unpredictable,

We must nevertheless note the potential for certain favourable changes, if only in view of the more evident interest of the West European states in . . . ensuring that the level of tension and confrontation does not reach the point of danger and in the long term reduces rather than increases.[16]

This kind of writing enabled Robbin Laird to conclude in 1985,

referring several times to Lukin's work, that 'the sense that Atlanticism is in irrevocable decline and the relative independence of Europe
is on the rise is at the core of Soviet analyses of France in particular
and of European security more generally'.[17]

(b) Western Europe as a loyal ally

As time passed, the version which emphasized resistance to the
Reagan administration's policies inside the alliance became increasingly difficult to sustain. Cruise and Pershing-II deployment went
ahead at the end of 1983, SDI was endorsed by most of the allied
leaders, COCOM restrictions were tightened, export credits were
cut. West European states were induced to embark on military
intervention in Africa and the Middle East.

A number of dedicated strong Europeanists persisted with their
original interpretation. Writers like Knyazhinsky predicted that
'political realism would eventually prevail' in the countries of the
European Community. In July 1985 the then IMEMO Director
Aleksandr Yakovlev maintained that the heightening of East-West
tension had not, as it had in the past, led to a muting of conflicts
inside NATO. At the end of 1986 he was still writing, even if less
categorically, about intensifying 'centrifugal tendencies' inside the
Western alliance. He claimed that the new flexibility of Soviet
foreign policy had 'illuminated the depth and acuteness of current
inter-imperialist contradictions'.[18] As a rule, the accounts which
stressed conflict tended to start from the level of international
economic relations. Yakovlev, for instance, stated that as the United
States lost its postwar economic dominance, it tried to maintain its
position by using its persisting military hegemony. This would
inevitably lead to mounting political tensions in the alliance, as the
underlying factors of material interest asserted themselves.[19]

The majority view rested on a more political analysis. Several
specialists reported a strengthening of underlying conservative and
Atlanticist tendencies in Western Europe, 'also at the level of a
section of public opinion'.[20] They explained it as an effect of the
swing to the right in domestic politics and of the day-to-day
workings of intergovernmental institutions such as NATO, the
IMF, OECD, COCOM, and so on. A growing sense of interdependence and vulnerability, encouraged by mounting global problems and by the prevailing atmosphere of East-West tension, was

also identified as a factor encouraging solidarity. Yury Davydov wrote in 1986 that the widespread perception of military dependence on the United States played a crucial part. Ruling circles in Western Europe, he acknowledged, were very close to Washington on East-West relations issues 'and, assuming the persistence of the current atmosphere, will continue to be so in future'.[21]

Soviet authors are now able to write much more openly than was possible even two or three years ago about the 'Soviet threat' as a reality in the minds of the Western public. This has dramatically improved the coherence of their accounts of alliance politics. At the beginning of 1988 the deputy head of the Department of International Relations at IMEMO undoubtedly surprised many of his Soviet readers by informing them that the USSR is seen in the West as 'a fundamentally and profoundly hostile concentration of political and military power, inclined to expansion and to the manipulation of military force as the main instrument for attaining its ends'. In Europe, he continued, 'the thesis of a supposed existing Soviet superiority in conventional arms is an important element of Western political thinking', and leads to a preoccupation with preserving the American nuclear guarantee. 'Shifts in the balance of forces' in Africa, Asia and Latin America, he noted, had encouraged centripetal tendencies and provoked an impressive display of alliance unity and security cooperation.[22]

Different writers drew their own conclusions from events. For some they demonstrated yet again the continuing decisive role of American power. Others took the opportunity to deride earlier talk of the imminent collapse of NATO, and to assert that 'in the acute conflict of two tendencies in inter-imperialist relations, the first, unifying tendency has the upper hand'. In 1986, noting that in recent years Western Europe had 'left no noticeable trace in world affairs', Yury Davydov commented that doubts were beginning to surface about whether announcements of the emergence of a new power-centre in the 1970s had not perhaps been premature.[23]

Military integration in a NATO framework

Although defence specialists like Kolosov may have been prepared to speculate in the first half of the 1980s about the political consequences of greater West European military integration, they never really departed from the traditional Soviet view that, whatever progress was made in this field, things would remain firmly under the control of the United States.[24] The underlying reasons were political ones – lack of unity inside Western Europe, and a strengthening of transatlantic ties caused by the deterioration of East-West relations. These two factors, he judged, were 'unlikely to alter in the foreseeable future'.[25] In 1985 he emphasized that European military cooperation had made progress only in the sphere of procurement, and even that was limited. In the search for an institutional framework for broader collaboration, Western European Union (WEU), the NATO Eurogroup and the European Programme Group had all turned out to be inappropriate, whether for reasons of membership or limitations on their competence. Repeating a frequently stated Soviet view, he wrote: 'The defence policy area has been and remains fundamentally the domain of the national governments and NATO . . . in which the determining role is played by the United States.'[26]

The outcome of alliance debates over the Strategic Defence Initiative evoked a strong response in Moscow. Divergent defence and military-technological priorities in the West European capitals were seen to have played a decisive role. All the major West European powers, it was agreed, saw SDI as destabilizing, as a troublesome complication in arms control and as a long-term threat to regional security. But all had been drawn into participation at one level or another.[27] As for the 'European Defence Initiative' project, as it was termed, it was considered to be unlikely to prosper, except possibly under American tutelage:

> In spite of the reference being made in connection with the projected EDI to the need to attain Western Europe's unity in order to strengthen its position, and increase its influence on the USA, the actual purpose is primarily to invigorate military cooperation of the West European countries as NATO's 'European bulwark.'[28]

Such defence cooperation as did occur, it was being emphasized by virtually all writers by the middle of the decade, would be unlikely to work against Washington's interests. In 1986 it was observed that the resurrection of the WEU two years earlier had coincided with the first deployment of cruise and Pershing-II missiles, that the event had been greeted with enthusiasm by the most ardent supporters of Atlantic solidarity, and that one of the revitalized body's first steps thereafter had been to remove restraints on arms production by West Germany.[29] NATO's strategy was perceived as one of redistributing spending in the alliance, achieving a more effective division of labour, and strengthening Western Europe's military identity in a way which took away from the anti-American appeal of the peace movements.

Some feared that West European defence activism would open the door to a resurgence of German militarism. In the writing on the subject, the view was commonly expressed that, if this happened, responsibility would lie at the door of the United States. In 1984, when the idea that the Western alliance was loosening was still to be encountered, the journalist Ernst Genri had written:

> What will happen if the United States in the future, as a result of its mindless betting of everything in the international arena, begins to weaken, to lose initiative, to forfeit its influence on its allies . . .? To think that West German militarism is dead would be flippant. It is alive, waiting its time.[30]

In 1985, by contrast, Aleksandr Yakovlev revealed the limits of his sanguine view of growing West European independent-mindedness in a long article for the USA Institute journal, tracing the history of American support for German expansionism and Nazism. He drew attention to the elaborate network of security arrangements linking the United States with its most important ally in Europe. 'The military preparations of the FRG significantly exceed its defensive requirements,' he declared, 'but they are organically embedded in America's militaristic plans.'[31]

Thus America's allies in NATO were consistently urged to seek their salvation, neither in Atlantic solidarity nor in self-reliance, but in pan-European security agreements of the kind promoted by the USSR. In 1985 Kolosov stated that the period since 1970 had shown that, in whatever framework military cooperation took place, 'the end result has been a growth in the level of confrontation'.[32]

A continuing influence for moderation

It would be wrong to make too much of these shifts in the balance of perceptions. Despite Davydov's sceptical remark casting doubt on the existence of a West European power-centre, his writing as a whole reflected the belief that the region would in due course renew its drive towards greater autonomy.[33] It was not generally considered that the underlying changes in alliance relations which occurred in the 1970s had been reversed. Even writers of a strongly Atlanticist persuasion acknowledged the importance of political tensions inside NATO, with the West Europeans pursuing their own 'more or less independent Ostpolitik', opposing crusading anti-communism as well as trends to isolationism, and pushing Reagan to reopen the dialogue with Moscow after the tension surrounding the start of INF deployment in 1983. Soviet authors continued to describe West European public and leadership opinion as an important restraint on Washington's freedom of manoeuvre. The United States, they noted, could not afford to push its policy of confrontation too far, for fear of opening up lines of strain in the alliance. Pressures to revive detente would eventually become so strong, wrote Davydov in 1986, that Washington would be forced to go along with them or become isolated.[34]

A special role was allotted by some specialists to West European Social-Democratic and Socialist parties. They were declared to have undergone a substantial change in attitude during the period of detente and to have become much more resistant to American pressure than they had been in the 1960s, partly because of competition from peace movements. There were enthusiastic reports of critical comments made by British and West German opposition leaders about the Reagan administration's policies, and even Mitterrand was given credit for his firm line on the gas pipeline dispute of 1982 and his criticism of SDI. It was noted that 'a number of the largest opposition parties' had been particularly receptive to Gorbachev's attempts to break down hostile stereotypes of the USSR, and had changed their platforms accordingly.[35]

This picture fits well with the assumption which emerges even more forcefully from writing in the strong Europeanist mode, that it is the United States, rather than the West as a whole, which is the seat of hostility to the Soviet Union. Like Kissinger, whose response to German Ostpolitik was 'to channel the inevitable in the desired direction', Reagan, in Shein's account, was forced to appear to endorse detente primarily as a way of controlling his alliance partners. Greater independent-mindedness on the part of America's allies was therefore virtually by definition a good thing, and was to be encouraged at every opportunity.[36]

Even in 1987, Davydov was interpreting in an optimistic sense the growing tensions set off inside NATO by the warming of Soviet-American relations. By shaking confidence in the American nuclear guarantee, he wrote, Reykjavik had increased West European independent-mindedness, which was also bolstered by the EC's geographical enlargement and by its new-found economic and technological dynamism. The author concluded that it was 'the spectre of Rapallo' which had forced the United States to modify its stance, and that both halves of the alliance were finding their partnership increasingly irksome.[37]

There is a note of caution in this article, however, that echoes a more general feeling of uneasiness which was growing among Soviet foreign affairs specialists, namely that European help in improving East-West relations had perhaps been taken too much for granted.

(c) Western Europe: threats and opportunities

It was becoming obvious by 1987, after all, that changes in Soviet-American relations were quite capable of transforming the political landscape inside the Atlantic alliance in unwelcome ways. As the IMEMO journal expressed it some time later:

> Towards the middle of the 1980s a definite shift took place in the foreign policy of the United States. Soviet-American talks on nuclear and space weapons got under way, and the leadership dialogue was resumed. All this reduced somewhat the anxiety of West European and Japanese politicians about Washington's confrontational line. But there immediately began to emerge a new set of contradictions in the security sphere.[38]

In the face of what they pictured as a new obstructiveness in London and Paris, Soviet writers were obliged to take a fresh look at the role of Western Europe in international affairs.

By the mid-1980s, specialist authors had begun to exploit the greater freedom of expression allowed to them in order to produce accounts of the defence debates inside NATO which were remarkably similar in some respects to those published in the West. Washington, so the analysis ran, responded to its loss of strategic superiority over the USSR with a purposeful drive to obtain larger contributions to the defence effort from its partners, thereby increasing 'the combined military capacity of imperialism'; to regain areas of strategic superiority; to provide for a pattern of escalation which reduced the early vulnerability of its own territory; and to enhance NATO cohesiveness. Its allies, by contrast, pursued reactive and 'contradictory' policies. They strove to restrain risky or provocative aspects of American policy, while doing everything possible to avoid decoupling, and to preserve the nuclear guarantee. They were reluctant, it was noted, to spend enough to meet American demands for burden-sharing, far less to achieve greater self-sufficiency and autonomy. They were constrained by the need to avoid provoking pacifist and anti-American feeling in their populations. European support for the deployment of cruise and Pershing-II missiles, the guarded attitude to their removal, the opposition to limited nuclear war, space defence and no-first-use proposals were all explained in these terms.[39]

As already indicated, defence policy in Western Europe was perceived in Moscow as a matter for NATO and national governments. The absence of a regional security identity meant that in this area, in contrast with other spheres, the United States was able to maintain a pattern of bilateral relations with European capitals. Soviet writers therefore found it necessary to devote a good deal of attention to the separate national security policies of the main West European states and their place in the alliance.

The United Kingdom aroused less interest in this respect than the other major West European powers. Its stance was considered to be more predictably Atlanticist and difficult to influence. Despite hints of a reorientation towards European defence cooperation under Edward Heath, and attempts to cut military expenditure in the mid-1970s, despite persistent support for a continuation of arms control, and foot-dragging on SDI during the 1980s, British policy was perceived as consistently dedicated to preserving NATO unity and London's own key position in the alliance.[40]

French defence policy and West European military cooperation
In 1985 Soviet writers were still giving credit to France for its pioneering role in promoting Europeanist attitudes and detente. Deputy Foreign Minister Anatoly Kovalev seemed reluctant to part with earlier favourable images, maintaining that even President Mitterrand, 'whose devotion to Atlanticism is well-known', had preserved a good deal of independence in foreign affairs, as

demonstrated by his critical attitude to the Strategic Defence Initiative.[41] However, by this time the general tone of Soviet references to France had been thoroughly soured by a series of events which appeared to indicate that Gaullist *tous azimuths* strategic rhetoric had been buried for good. Mitterrand had intervened in German politics, and had thrown his weight behind the deployment of cruise and Pershing-II missiles. He had rejected Gorbachev's proposals for reducing and removing nuclear weapons in Europe, and showed no signs of willingness to cut his own rocket forces even after the first-stage 50 per cent Soviet and American reductions envisaged in START. French conventional forces were described in Moscow as 'an integral component of NATO forces in Europe', France's nuclear strategy was seen to be coming closer to that of its allies, and its Europeanism was said to be evolving down the unwelcome path of encouraging military cooperation with the Germans, even if this meant colluding in German military expansion.[42]

In 1988 Nikolai Afanasevsky, like Kovalev in his own earlier career a leading French specialist in the Soviet Foreign Ministry, acknowledged that Franco-Soviet relations could no longer be described as privileged or exemplary. After Mitterrand's visit to Moscow in 1984, he wrote: 'We had the impression that things were gradually normalizing.' But Paris's subsequent actions had disappointed these hopes. Lately, he complained, France had been the most active proponent of maintaining the American military presence in Europe and reinforcing the European pillar of NATO. Its Europeanism was also of a dangerous kind: 'What is one to make of the fact that France and the Federal Republic of Germany are increasingly militarizing their cooperation? What or whom are these efforts directed against?' French and British plans to modernize their strategic nuclear arsenals could substantially alter the balance of forces in the European theatre. It was an urgent matter, he considered, to seek mutual understanding with the French on security issues.[43]

The events of 1987 and 1988 were clearly forcing another reconsideration of the prospects for military integration in Western Europe. At a round-table discussion held in 1987, Kolosov and likeminded experts still argued that Atlanticist structures and attitudes continued to dominate in the security sphere. The overall prospects for European military collaboration they described as 'nebulous in the extreme'.[44] But other participants disagreed, asserting that the process was 'not in the least stagnating', but had advanced to new, higher levels in the 1980s, with thirty kinds of weapon jointly developed or under development in 1986. One maintained that Western Europe's growing defence industry was encouraging 'military-technological polycentrism', and changing the balance of forces inside the alliance.[45]

In May 1988 a senior Foreign Ministry official wrote in the journal *International Affairs*:

> The revival of the military articles of the 1963 Elysée Treaty
> with the FRG, the stepped-up military cooperation with
> Britain, Italy and Spain, the reanimation of Western European
> Union, the Platform for European Security Interests adopted in
> the Hague – all these and other integrational processes in
> Western Europe have been inspired and organized mainly by
> Paris, which clearly is looking for a 'European' political justifi-
> cation of its policy of perpetuating 'nuclear deterrence' ... Paris
> urges the adoption of the idea of military integration in the
> system of the European Community, which in the future will be
> transformed into a European Union and at the first stage will
> be a confederation with supranational policy and defence and
> then, perhaps, a superpower, something like a United States of
> Europe. This is the mood spreading among the younger genera-
> tion in the countries of the European Community.[46]

The forceful, and some might say exaggerated, tone of these reports is probably evidence of a struggle which was going on inside the Soviet foreign affairs community over the direction of policy. The campaign for a more European orientation also involved a more thoroughgoing analysis of the strategic concerns of the West European states. At the end of 1987 the defence specialist Sergei Karaganov (now a deputy director of the Institute for the Study of Europe) wrote at length about the sense of vulnerability felt by Washington's European partners. These feelings were intensified, he explained, by geopolitical factors: by the lack of 'strategic depth' in the West, by 'certain aspects of the force structure' of the Warsaw Pact, and its large numbers of tanks, by the pattern of military manoeuvres, by the character of Soviet military doctrine, and by the habitual psychology of confrontation. Things had improved since

1985, but the Soviet Union was still widely perceived as threatening, and for that reason the Europeans resisted 'decoupling' from the United States at all costs.[47]

The implication of all this was that Soviet policy-makers had been at fault, as leading officials up to and including Shevardnadze were to admit, in 'underestimating' and neglecting Europe.[48] By now it was possible for three Foreign Ministry specialists to state the case quite baldly:

> US monopoly on engaging in dialogue with the USSR consolidates American leadership in the West, leaving Western Europe a secondary role in world politics. In our view, we largely facilitated this ourselves. Bewitched by the industrial and military might of the United States, we failed to notice, or – to be more precise – did not take fully into account, the fact that Pax Americana was shaking and had begun to crumble, while other imperialist centres, including Western Europe, were becoming more active in world affairs. Meanwhile we continued to think in the strategic categories of global parity and stability, above all with regard to Soviet-American relations, not paying the French and British nuclear forces the amount of attention their strategic capability deserved.[49]

The authors also raised again the option of coming to terms with the tendency to military integration in the West of the continent, in order to influence its consequences. The political-military bloc which is taking shape, they wrote, is capable of evolving either as a European pillar of NATO, or as 'a means of influencing the USA, an organization for expressing special interests of West Europeans, different from US interests'. The second outcome is likely, the authors continued, only if the USSR 'takes due account of the Europeans' growing striving for greater independence in security matters, and if the Europeans are offered a chance to begin a search for new, mutually acceptable ways of determining their place in the European and world strategic balance'.[50]

The senior ministry employee entrusted with the task of replying to this paper acknowledged that there was a degree of truth in the criticism of Americano-centrism, but claimed that this had never been allowed to go too far. More significantly, he dissociated himself from the implication that there were only two security options for

Western Europe, and that the Europeanist one must be encouraged. Reasserting the official line that there was a 'third way', he wrote:

> The growth of military integration in Western Europe and creation of some new organizational forms of a 'European buttress' of NATO may provide Western Europe with yet another instrument for influencing the USA. But a far more essential and really negative result of this will be that the split of Europe into opposed blocs will be consolidated and new obstacles will be put up in the general European process and the construction of a common European home will be impeded, to the detriment of our interests as well. That is why we are so concerned over the military-integration tendencies in Western Europe. They are of concern to us also because open and secret plans for continuing the modernization of weapons and the arms race and the perpetuation of nuclear deterrence may be the result of these tendencies.[51]

This more hopeful view, that a way out could be found by dismantling the East-West confrontation in Europe, was supported by a number of specialists. Karaganov, for instance, wrote that solid progress had already been made as a result of Gorbachev's new thinking in East-West relations. West European governments had not after all moved energetically to develop the new generation of powerful and accurate conventional weapons required to implement NATO's deep-strike strategy. They no doubt realized that they would be both costly and destabilizing. 'There is an increasing tendency', he wrote, 'to seek a way out based on arms reductions.' Moscow's 'bold and decisive' actions had encouraged public opposition to nuclear weapons. It was defeat in regional elections during the summer which had encouraged Chancellor Kohl to stop opposing the elimination of the Pershing-IA missiles and thereby remove the last obstacle to the INF deal. At government level too, he concluded, 1987 had shown that 'traditional stereotypes are being revised and new prospects for lowering the level of confrontation opened up'.[52]

The fruits of European diplomacy
It was not just in order to avoid the risks associated with greater West European assertiveness in the defence sphere that greater

'Europeanism' in Soviet foreign policy was being advocated in 1987 and 1988; more positive incentives were being pointed to as well. Like Karaganov, many writers emphasized the effect of Soviet disarmament initiatives in shrinking the perception of a threat from the East among the West European public, and the way in which governments, especially the West German one, were already modifying their position.

During the Soviet/West German diplomatic freeze which began in 1984, specialist commentary on German policy had been sparse and had been restricted largely to amplifying and documenting official complaints. These concerned, first, 'the strong US accent in Bonn's policy', evident for instance in its support for the SDI project and its energetic role in NATO's conventional arms modernization plans; and, second, Germany's attempts to exploit West European military cooperation for its own ends. A sharp line was drawn between 'constructive', 'realistic' elements (in the anti-nuclear movement, in the SPD and, to a degree, in the FDP) and revanchist and militarist ones (in the defence complex and the CDU/CSU).[53]

After the Kohl administration had played its part in bringing the INF negotiations to a successful conclusion in the autumn of 1987, it began to look as if West Germany was being welcomed back, bit by bit, to the special relationship with the USSR which had existed prior to 1983. Foreign affairs experts enjoyed greater freedom to analyse Soviet-German relations. By the autumn of 1988 the IMEMO journal's Bonn correspondent was able to declare that 'the positions of the Soviet Union and the Federal Republic of Germany are close or coincide on a whole string of the most important international issues'. It was stated that Moscow and Bonn had common interests in cutting strategic rocket arsenals, removing rather than modernizing tactical nuclear weapons, achieving agreement on substantial reductions in conventional arms in Europe, banning chemical weapons, expanding East-West trade and technological cooperation, and easing COCOM restrictions on technology transfer.[54]

Asked to explain in February 1988 why Bonn's position had 'changed so sharply and so rapidly', the CPSU International Department's deputy head, Vadim Zagladin, responded that one should look, rather, for continuity with well-established FDP/SPD policy. The Kohl government had, after all, always affirmed its intention of persisting with its predecessors' line. 'Admittedly there were certain retreats and waverings,' Zagladin continued, but the West German leaders had come to realize that these were counter-productive. Specialist writers pointed to more immediate factors. They noted that the turnover of generations meant that those who had grown up to accept the postwar frontiers of Germany were having an increasing influence on policy. Soviet disarmament proposals and internal reforms had had an enormous impact on the electorate, and strengthened already powerful ecological and peace movements. The principal opposition party, the SPD, had pursued a consistently 'constructive' foreign policy line and had been rewarded with increasing popularity among the voters. The FDP and its leader, Hans-Dietrich Genscher, had acted as an authoritative voice of realism inside the ruling coalition.[55]

It was commented that Bonn had now endorsed the slogan of a 'Common European Home'. This was so, Soviet authors explained, not just because the Germans appreciated that the division of their nation was inseparable from the division of the continent; it also reflected long-standing interests in developing a closer commercial relationship with their Eastern neighbours.[56] As Margarita Maksimova at IMEMO pointed out, West German business circles were particularly keen to gain access to new markets in 1987 and 1988. The Deutschmark was overvalued against the dollar, trade with the developing world was hampered by debt problems, unemployment remained high, and there was an urgent need to find ways of paying off recent large investments in research and development.[57]

How should the USSR respond in such circumstances? There was some division of opinion. Reviewing changing German attitudes in April 1988, the *Pravda* commentator V. Mikhailov wrote: 'Some people have seen all these innovations as the run-in to a fundamental change, while others have seen them only as a modification of the old claims.'[58] Maksimova displayed few such doubts, and made an eloquent case for taking advantage of what she described as the unique military, economic and ecological situation in Europe, in order to move Soviet/West German relations on to a new level. The Federal Republic, she argued, possesses an enormous economic and technological potential. Manfred Woerner's appointment as NATO Secretary-General highlighted the way in which the increased attention being given to conventional arms and short-range nuclear weapons was enhancing West Germany's role in NATO politics. A string of processes at work in the European Community – the building of the Single Market, military integration, heightened political cooperation, the strengthening of supranational features – all reflected the Federal Republic's preferences and would in turn increase its influence in Brussels.

In Maksimova's view, the USSR had the opportunity to improve relations with Bonn in a number of ways. In the military sphere, it could speed up the elaborating and implementing of non-offensive doctrine, foster contacts between military personnel on both sides, and form joint German-Soviet research groups. In the political sphere, it could work together with the Germans to develop a more precise conception of the Common European Home and a detailed programme for putting it into practice. In the economic sphere, it could experiment with free-trade zones, German-equipped science parks in Soviet university towns, new commercial structures and new types of trading enterprise.[59]

Her IMEMO colleague Yudanov warned, however, that it would be premature to conclude that the new thinking had become solidly entrenched in Bonn – old positions were still being defended by the ruling coalition on tactical nuclear weapons, the denuclearization of Europe and other arms issues. He and other writers warned that powerful elements in the governing parties still cherished unrealistic aspirations to national reunification. One went so far as to link this with 'interference in the affairs of other states and exporting counter-revolution', for example in the GDR, Poland, the Baltic republics and Azerbaijan.[60]

Another important qualification was made by Zagladin, in a television interview in February 1988. The new 'realistic' tendencies in Bonn's foreign policy, he explained, stem from its desire to find a path for exercising political influence commensurate with the country's economic potential, but 'this does not mean that the FRG is retreating from NATO or from the alliance with the United States'.[61] During the second half of the 1980s, foreign affairs specialists in Moscow had become keenly aware of the capacity of individual West European states to intervene actively in East-West security relations, for good or for ill. It had become clear that there were substantial rewards to be reaped, and penalties to be avoided, by taking careful account of national aspirations and preoccupations. But in the earlier part of the decade the lesson had been taught that the activities of NATO's European members were unlikely to stray beyond the boundaries set by a deeply rooted sense of dependence on the alliance.

(d) Summary

The balance of Soviet expert perceptions of Western Europe's role in East-West relations can be described as having passed through three phases in the course of the 1980s. Each new stage was marked by the shedding of over-optimistic assumptions.

The first phase coincided broadly with the period in office of the first Reagan administration. The dominant version at this time was that West European independent-mindedness and attachment to the benefits of detente would prevail against American attempts to raise the level of East-West confrontation. By the middle of the decade, however, allied cooperation in INF deployment, in plans for conventional arms modernization, in the launching of the SDI project and in other areas had provoked a reassessment. This introduced a second phase, when transatlantic bonds were seen still to be more powerful, particularly in matters connected with security, than tendencies to autonomy. Foreign affairs writers began to acknowledge the importance of fear of a Soviet threat as a factor underpinning NATO unity.

Both in the first and in the second phase it was taken for granted that Western Europe would naturally act as a force for moderation in the alliance. In the third phase, by contrast, from 1987, it became understood that improving superpower relations could provoke a reallocation of roles. It was seen that America's European partners could determinedly oppose particular disarmament moves, could resist denuclearization of the continent, and indeed could make plans for a substantial expansion of their own strategic arsenals. European defence cooperation, which had never been taken particularly seriously by Soviet observers, now appeared in a much more threatening light.

Because of the greater openness of discussion which was possible in the second half of the 1980s, it rapidly became clear that this third phase of perceptions was accompanied by a campaign to strengthen the 'European direction' in Soviet foreign policy. It was argued, first, that the mid-1980s focus on negotiations with the United States had been excessive and that Moscow's neglect for West European security concerns had damaged Soviet interests. In the second place it was emphasized that there were substantial rewards to be derived from cultivating relations with Western Europe.

The transition from phase one to phase two marked a setback for the 'strong Europeanist' position, which stressed conflict and centrifugal tendencies inside the Western alliance, and the potential for independent action of 'realistic', detente-inclined forces on the continent. It strengthened the 'moderate Europeanist' view that, although there is a long-term trend to greater relative weight and autonomy for Western Europe in NATO, this is not likely to have dramatic effects in international affairs in the near term, in view of the continued tenacity of Atlanticist attitudes. It also harmonized with the broader underlying tendency described in Chapters 2 and 3 to emphasize more strongly the force of interdependence, both in the world in general and in the Atlantic community in particular. Events appeared to reinforce the perception of Western Europe as a junior partner, able to exert a restraining influence, but a long way from threatening revolt or departure, even if it had wanted to.

By casting doubt on assumptions common to both tendencies about West European 'constructiveness' and 'realism', the events which ushered in the third phase encouraged what might be called a 'sober Europeanism'. The distinguishing characteristic of this position was a much keener awareness of the potential constructive or destructive impact of decisions taken in Western Europe on the course of East-West relations and of the need for the USSR to act energetically to influence these decisions.

5
GORBACHEV'S EUROPEAN POLICY

(a) New thinking

Changes in Soviet attitudes to Western Europe and Soviet policy in the region are part of the wider influx of 'new thinking' at the top level in the mid-1980s. From one point of view this was only the latest stage in a process which was not itself new, but had been going on for the preceding thirty years. During this time revised versions of the established Soviet world-view, put together by international affairs experts, had painfully and unevenly been penetrating into the language of decision-makers.

Official thinking has tended to advance in a series of shifts, provoked by changes in domestic and world politics. These shifts have normally been accompanied, as in the mid-1950s and late 1960s, by moves to strengthen the institutional basis of foreign policy research. At each stage, however, established perspectives and interests offered powerful resistance to innovation.

During the Brezhnev years, it appears that the leadership did little to resolve the contradictions which this process gave rise to. Debate and consultation were compartmentalized, different institutions pursued conflicting policies, and top-level statements reflected the underlying incoherence.[1] The General Secretary endorsed radical innovations in doctrine and policy associated with East-West detente, arms control and economic cooperation. Simultaneously he lent his support to an ambitious programme of military expansion and global intervention which accorded with the aspirations of the armed forces and the kind of optimistic hopes for building alliances with 'progressive forces' in the Third World which were no longer being taken seriously by the majority of specialist observers. Whatever the reason – political weakness, bureaucratic resistance or simply inertia – the upshot was that, in the combining of cooperation and competition with the West, the balance tended to be struck predominantly with an eye to immediate competitive advantage.[2]

By the time that a new generation came to power with Gorbachev, the ineffectiveness of the Brezhnev strategy had been thoroughly demonstrated. In the United States the most hostile administration since the years of the Cold War had been elected and re-elected. NATO unity had been enhanced, and a new, costly and technologically challenging spiral of the arms race was under way. Trade, especially technology transfer, was languishing under political restrictions, and economic growth was slowing down. In the Western world popular sympathy for the Soviet Union, even on the left, was at a low ebb. Involvement in the Third World had turned out in most cases to be expensive and unsuccessful (notably in Afghanistan). Moscow, like Washington ten years before, was aware that the costs of maintaining hegemony by military means were beyond its economic capabilities.[3] The consequence was a fairly comprehensive victory for the moderates. Those second-rank figures who had fought for policies of negotiation, arms control and conciliation during the 1970s found themselves promoted to senior positions in the Foreign Ministry (Petrovsky, Kovalev) and in the Party foreign affairs apparatus (Dobrynin, Shakhnazarov), or appointed as research institute directors (Primakov, Zhurkin). The institutional representation and status of the military were downgraded, and new national security concepts, such as 'reasonable sufficiency' and 'non-offensive defence' were endorsed by military leaders.[4]

Detente was now no longer explained as a consequence of Western weakness in the 'correlation of world forces'. Compromises could be struck, according to the new version, because both sides were becoming aware of the need to put 'all-human interests' above class interests. It was not just that nuclear war was seen as a suicidal option. Interdependence – security, ecological, financial – was being experienced as a more and more powerful constraint. The militarism which Lenin had described as a central characteristic of twentieth-century capitalism was now plainly counterproductive: security could be ensured only by negotiation and by agreements which respected the rights and concerns of both sides. 'Export of revolution' and 'matching American steps in the arms race' were rejected in principle, and previous policies, such as intervention in Afghanistan and large-scale deployment of SS-20s, were criticized by spokesmen close to the leadership.[5]

Underlying this change of stance is the realization that the Soviet Union's competitive potential is smaller than had been pretended. Inessential commitments around the world must therefore be shed. The number of sites of confrontation must be reduced, and its general level lowered. The aim is to restore foreign policy to 'profitability'.[6] New alliances must be forged wherever likely political and economic benefits, rather than short-term military advantage, dictate. In the East-West relationship rewards must be maximized and costs reduced.

Recent doctrinal innovations are well matched to such a situation. In the first place, they make virtues of necessities. By advocating flexibility in negotiation and 'reasonable sufficiency' in weaponry as imperatives of the nuclear age, Gorbachev minimizes the impression at home of a humiliating climbdown, and lays the foundation for transforming the USSR's image abroad without an obvious show of weakness.[7] Secondly, as we have seen, there has been a growing awareness in Moscow of how deeply entrenched have become hostile and apprehensive feelings towards the Soviet Union in other countries. If security is a matter of politics, and trust, then it is a task of the highest priority to break down what Soviet spokesmen call 'enemy images' and 'stereotypes'. Here again, changes in doctrine have an important part to play. The emphasis on environmental deterioration, poverty and other 'global problems', and the use of the concept of interdependence, appeal to a Western informed public who have been familiar with such ideas since the 1970s, and help to reinforce a well-intentioned, idealistic image, a long way from the hard-faced intransigence which the USSR projected in earlier years.[8] The emphasis on multipolarity in international affairs also represents a recycling of Western ideas. It makes it easier for the Soviet Union to extract itself from regional conflicts, and easier to criticize the United States for becoming involved in them.

Yet too broad an appeal to public opinion in the West can be counterproductive. All-out Soviet backing for the unsuccessful campaign to prevent cruise and Pershing-II deployment played into the hands of Western governments, who managed to use it as a way of discrediting internal opposition. It was also noted that the population appeared to be very susceptible to persuasion by right-wing populist campaigning in the mass media.[9] The Gorbachev administration has accordingly put more emphasis on influencing the thinking of Western decision-makers and advisers. State-to-state relations, it insists, are to be kept quite separate from ideological or class conflict.[10] It has striven to increase the number of government and expert-level forums of discussion. It has adopted a reasonable, matter-of-fact tone, shorn of any traces of the calcified revolutionary rhetoric of the Brezhnev period. Finally, it has shown a readiness to make real concessions of the kind listed in Chapter 1. Left-of-centre politicians are still cultivated, especially if, as in Germany, they have the prospect of coming to power, but Gorbachev has moved decisively to reach an understanding with the key conservative leaders – Reagan, Thatcher, Strauss.[11]

(b) The approach to the alliance

In this framework of priorities, an opening to Europe made good sense in 1985. The Reagan administration's policies had heightened transatlantic tensions around strategic and trade aspects of East-West relations, creating opportunities for Soviet diplomacy. Even the *Izvestiya* commentator Aleksandr Bovin, who remained optimistic about the medium-term prospects for relations with Washington, wrote: 'Europe is the cradle of detente, and the rebirth of detente will be simpler to attain in Europe than anywhere else.'[12] Western Europe was perceived in Moscow both as the principal site of military danger and as the main partner in economic cooperation. In both these areas there had been substantial but avoidable setbacks. A correcting of defensive overinsurance by the USSR might yield dramatic improvements in the political atmosphere, with immediate consequences for trade and scientific and technological cooperation. Western Europe might be used, as it had been fifteen years before, to draw the United States into detente.

Perceptions

Were there other arguments in the minds of Soviet policy-makers, arguments which held out the possibility of exploiting shifts in the balance of power inside the Western alliance to displace the United States from its postwar role in Europe? Speculation of this kind might easily have been encouraged by the 'strong Europeanism' of figures like Aleksandr Yakovlev, which stressed the decline of American hegemony and mounting transatlantic conflict over East-West relations. However, the specialist literature reviewed in Chapters 2–4 suggests that if such scenarios were promoted at all, it was by a small minority. During the mid-1980s Soviet observers were adjusting downwards their estimates of Western Europe's powers of resistance to American pressure, and its capacity for pursuing an independent foreign policy, especially in East-West relations.

It was acknowledged that long-term trends to the evening-out of economic potentials of the various 'imperialist power-centres' can encompass fairly lengthy periods of relative economic decline in Western Europe. It was also admitted that changes in the correlation of economic forces are not necessarily translated into shifts in political relations: great-power status depends on a whole set of factors, and economic giants can remain political pygmies.[13] Underlying all this is a set of widely held assumptions according to which the power of transnational corporations and international economic regulatory bodies is likely to increase, prolonging American dominance and damping down tendencies to self-assertion by competitors. This trend makes futile any strategy of attempting to concentrate contacts with the world economy in a particular region.

The limits of Western Europe's attachment to detente have come to be more clearly appreciated. It has been understood that fear of the Soviet Union and apprehensions about possible decoupling from the United States can act as a virtually irresistible stimulus to alliance discipline. The tensions of the early 1980s were seen to have encouraged Atlantic unity, and what one writer called 'a mutual interpenetration of Europeanism and Atlanticism'. Baranovsky summed up the situation as follows:

'Atlanticism' can thus be thought of as emphasizing solidarity between the United States and Western Europe, while not excluding West European autonomy. 'Europeanism', on the other hand, assumes an emphasis on the autonomy of the integration community, but at the same time does not exclude solidarity with the United States.[14]

Thus Gorbachev was not necessarily attempting to mislead his hosts when he declared to the French National Assembly in October 1985 that the USSR fully respected the stability of the 'historical, political and economic relations' which linked Western Europe and the United States.[15]

In the second half of the decade, British and French reactions to the INF deal, and the speeding-up of West European military cooperation, rekindled Soviet awareness of the risks which were likely to accompany the opportunities of increasing multipolarity, and helped to give birth to a third phase in the development of perceptions. The European NATO allies could no longer be seen predominantly as more or less useful intermediaries for influencing American behaviour, but appeared instead as relatively independent actors who could upset simplistic, bilaterally framed calculations in East-West relations.

In February 1988 Vadim Zagladin acknowledged that many people had perceived the Reykjavik and Geneva summits as 'an attempt by the two great powers to bypass the Europeans and to reach some form of agreement behind their backs'.[16] By this time, with chemical and conventional weapons rising on the disarmament agenda, and with a thaw under way between Moscow and Bonn, a sense of urgency had begun to be reflected, in specialist and in official statements, about the need to pay more attention to the region. At a Foreign Ministry conference held in July 1988, Eduard Shevardnadze complained that, despite the wide-ranging repercussions in international affairs of progress towards greater integration in Western Europe, 'no one in a single division of the Ministry' was employed in forecasting its likely future course. In the conference section devoted to policy priorities, so it was reported, practically all the speakers acknowledged that 'the European sector ... has been pushed to the sidelines by our activity towards the United States'. They all 'came out for more vigorous contacts at all levels'.[17]

This change in perceptions represents a slight readjustment, of course, not a reversion to earlier illusions. The prevailing opinion at the Foreign Ministry conference was summed up in the words, 'If we are "targeted" on the United States, this is a reflection of objective reality.' It was also agreed by participants that 'no attempt to dissociate Western Europe from the United States could bear fruit'.[18]

Policies

Soviet policy-makers were at the same time quite well aware that there existed sufficient divergence of interests in the alliance to make it well worth while pursuing a policy of indirect leverage. On the eve of Gorbachev's departure for Paris in the autumn of 1985 Aleksandr Bovin stated in *Izvestiya* that Moscow intended 'to utilize Western Europe's potential to make good ... the obvious shortage of common sense in the present US administration'. Shortly afterwards, the Soviet Foreign Ministry publication *International Affairs* openly urged West European governments to 'suggest more realistic assessments and conclusions to the US leadership'.[19] Such 'spillover' tactics are a familiar feature of Soviet diplomacy in East-West relations. In a similar way Franco-Soviet relations were cultivated in the second half of the 1960s, and a series of favours granted to Paris, in order to encourage the West Germans to move ahead more rapidly with their new Ostpolitik.[20]

However, the characteristic feature of Gorbachev's use of leverage politics, as of his open diplomacy directed at the Western public, is that it is concerted with a genuine drive to reach agreements with the principal interlocutors. The General Secretary can advance his ambitious plans for disarmament, and for reducing the level of confrontation in Europe as in other regions, only by dealing directly with the other superpower. His Europeanist rhetoric should not be allowed to distract attention from the persistence with which he wooed the United States in 1985–7, in the face of repeated rebuffs.[21] Shevardnadze himself described as unprecedented the four US-Soviet summit meetings and twenty-eight meetings at foreign-minister level which were held during Gorbachev's first few years in office.

Separate disarmament offers made to the West European nuclear powers, meanwhile, were not of a kind to be taken seriously in London and Paris. For a long time the USSR insisted on including British and French missiles in an INF agreement. At the Reykjavik summit in October 1986 it lifted this condition but simultaneously relinked an agreement on regional nuclear disarmament with progress towards a deal on SDI, thereby revealing the essentially subsidiary role which Western Europe played in its arms control strategy. When in February 1987 Moscow again made the INF deal self-standing, Deputy Foreign Minister Vorontsov stated that his government 'also aimed at giving a positive impetus to work on other areas of the talks, namely on outer space and on strategic offensive armaments'.[22]

The emphasis on relations with London in the early years of Gorbachev's European diplomacy fits well with the idea that the USSR was interested first and foremost in exerting influence on the Americans. Conversely, the slowdown in relations with West Germany from 1984 to 1987 casts doubt on the seriousness of the 'European direction' of Soviet policy, given the Federal Republic's key position in East-West European economic relations and in the strategic pattern on the continent. It was to the West German Finance Minister in May 1988 that Gorbachev chose to make a veiled apology, when he declared that the Soviet Union had 'never, under any circumstances, relegated European affairs to the background, no matter what was said, despite claims that the USSR in relations with the West has other, preferable interests'.[23]

Chancellor Kohl's visit to Moscow in October of the same year was therefore an important signal that a more active regional diplomacy was at last under way. Intensive discussions were launched with West German business representatives and officials at various levels. Firm plans were made for a series of visits by Gorbachev to West European capitals in the first half of 1989 – to London, Paris, Bonn and Rome – the first to be undertaken since his isolated visit to Paris in 1985.

Welcome and unwelcome shifts in attitudes on East-West issues in France, Britain and West Germany in 1987 and 1988 clearly played a part in bringing about this change of policy. But there were other factors at work. The steady progress in EC-CMEA negotiations had finally produced an agreement between the two bodies (June 1988), and direct Soviet-EC talks were under way. The economic pressures on the USSR to exploit every opportunity for obtaining technological and industrial assistance from its Western neighbours were mounting visibly, and it was clear that decisive measures would have to be taken to stimulate flagging East-West trade. There was apprehension about the likely effects of the Single Market project, and there were hopes of gaining an entry to joint West European research-and-development programmes. Strategic arms talks with the United States were moving slowly, and not much progress was expected during the presidential election period. The spotlight in arms control was clearly on conventional arms in Europe. This pointed to a much more determined effort at consultation with the nations directly involved.

Politics

As the evidence of Soviet internal discussions indicates, this was an adjustment of policy, not a volte-face. Like the USA's European allies in the quotation from Baranovsky's book just cited, the USSR strives to combine 'Europeanism' and 'Atlanticism'. As in the West, the combination sometimes gives an ambivalent impression, and it accommodates rival political tendencies. In Moscow these tendencies must express themselves within the institutions of a single party, and sometimes inside the pages of a single party document. Thus the 27th Party Congress Political Report in 1986 contained an opening section 'The Contemporary World', which in the style of Aleksandr Yakovlev painted a picture of deepening inter-imperialist contradictions and declining American power. The fourth section, however, 'Basic Aims and Directions of the Party's Foreign Policy Strategy', dealt first and foremost with the prospects for improving relations with the United States. European affairs were treated only in passing, in one short paragraph out of sixty.

It is not difficult to trace a continuing debate. The Deputy Foreign Minister, Anatoly Kovalev, who managed the Soviet side of the Helsinki negotiations, persistently praised European independent-mindedness, maturity and tolerance in East-West relations, and painted a glowing future for pan-European cooperation. Valentin Falin, Kovalev's partner in the European diplomacy of the 1970s, and recently installed as head of the Party's International Department, continued to flay American 'neo-globalism': 'Friends are a nuisance for those who want to lord it over the world,' he wrote in 1986. 'Such people need servants, a retinue, a claque.'[24] At the same time other members of the Soviet foreign policy establishment seized on evidence that Washington's line was softening to hold out the prospect of large-scale, long-term cooperation between the USA and the USSR.[25]

The fact that Yakovlev, Falin and Kovalev were all promoted to more senior posts by Gorbachev early in his period in office must be balanced against the appointment of Anatoly Dobrynin, the very embodiment of Soviet-American rapport in the 1970s,[26] as head of the Party's International Department; Evgeny Primakov to replace Yakovlev as Director of IMEMO; and Vitaly Zhurkin as head of the new Academy of Sciences Institute of Europe. At the time of his appointment Zhurkin was one of the leading USA Institute Americanists. As some of the material cited in earlier chapters demonstrates, this is no guarantee of a partisan 'Atlanticism', but it is clear that, like many of his academic colleagues, he is immune to excessive Europeanist enthusiasm. He chose to begin a recent article on the future of Europe by commenting on the apparent untimeliness of the subject:

> Strangely enough, there is increasing talk about the unique future role of Europe now that the Soviet Union and the US are reaching agreements and that Japan and the entire Pacific area are playing a more important role. Indeed, Europe has dominated the world scene for two millennia, but in recent decades it has been visibly edged out by other centres of the globe.

It is possible, he conceded, that the region's efforts to regain momentum, through the Single Market project and the Eureka programme, may produce a new economic giant strong enough to rival the United States and willing to choose new partners, but 'the answers to these questions are in the future, the remote future, perhaps'.[27]

Thus the pattern of appointments, like the balance of perceptions and of policies, indicates a degree of open-mindedness about the medium to long term, but a cautious refusal to embrace over-optimistic assessments of the kind which led to foreign policy debacles in various spheres under Khrushchev and Brezhnev. The widening of the horizon of Soviet foreign policy, which has brought new approaches to countries like Israel, China and Japan as well as to Western Europe, is part of a long-overdue move in the direction of greater efficiency and flexibility. As the recent shift in emphasis towards Europe demonstrates, the policy machine is now capable of responding swiftly to circumstances and executing carefully measured changes of direction.

'Strong Europeanist' argumentation came to the fore in unusual conditions of extreme tension between Moscow and Washington, and strained relations inside the Atlantic alliance. The similarity of

Gorbachev's Europeanist language in 1984 and 1985 to Yakovlev's suggests that the future Politburo member and Party Secretary temporarily exerted an exceptional degree of influence on the new leader's thinking. As progress began to be made in superpower relations, as the West European power-centre failed to live up to its destiny, and as the new foreign policy staff found their places, policy statements tended to revert to something closer to the traditional orientation, albeit with a multipolar colouring.

By the end of 1988 something of a swing-back had occurred in the personnel area, as Yakovlev acquired the post of Chairman of the new Central Committee Foreign Affairs Commission and Falin replaced Dobrynin as head of the International Department. But Dobrynin was retained as a foreign policy adviser to the General Secretary. At the latter's meeting with representatives of the Trilateral Commission in January 1989, for instance, Dobrynin was present along with the USA Institute and IMEMO heads Arbatov and Primakov, as well as Yakovlev and Falin.[28]

Gorbachev's foreign policy is vigorous and imaginative. The Soviet leadership is striving to regain some control over the environment, after a period when it had become increasingly isolated. This requires radical changes of posture, which bring with them risks and uncertainty. In such circumstances stability has a high priority. It is easy to understand and take seriously Shevardnadze's assurance to the West German Foreign Minister in 1986 that he had no wish to undermine NATO: 'We are of the opinion that, given all the alliances that have taken shape, it is essential to strengthen those threads whose severance is fraught with the danger of severance of the world fabric.' Gorbachev is doubtless sincere, too, when he speaks of wanting to avoid 'chaos' in Europe.[29] The USSR has for a long time attached great importance to institution-building and formalized dialogue in East-West relations, not just as a means of legitimizing the European status quo, but also because of the opportunities which are created for communication, leverage and 'thread'-pulling. NATO is an important part of the institutional fabric, and poor communications in NATO can complicate Gorbachev's plans for disarmament in Europe, as the post-Reykjavik period demonstrated.[30]

As is often pointed out, the USSR derives other substantial advantages from the continued existence of the Atlantic alliance. Its own military presence and controls over Eastern Europe are justified, and NATO is considered a safer option than the unknown quantity of a (possibly German-dominated) West European military entity.[31] Best of all would be a neutral Western Europe, but that does not appear to be on the cards. Soviet foreign affairs specialists, and Soviet leaders too, recognize that tension binds alliances together and detente tends to loosen them. Their declared long-term goal is the dissolution of military blocs in Europe. But they appear neither to expect nor to desire any substantial changes in the foreseeable future.

Reviewing Soviet attitudes to Western Europe in 1976, one Western author concluded that Moscow was made apprehensive on the one hand by any prospect of close integration in the Atlantic alliance and on the other by the possibility of its European members emerging as a 'Third Force':

> If Soviet leaders believed that the middle ground between extremes was great and relatively stable, there would be no cause for concern. Evidently, however, they do not. They seem, in fact, to fear the lingering force of the first extreme and the possibility that, when it collapses, events will move rapidly towards the second extreme.[32]

In that case, the evidence of the 1980s indicates a substantial shift in perceptions, and a move away from zero-sum thinking both about East-West and about West-West relations. Soviet writers appreciate much more fully the roots of Western alliance unity and its likely durability. West European unity is declared to be compatible not only with North Atlantic solidarity, but also with pan-European cooperation. Thus Moscow may foment 'all-European conscious-ness' and play on divisions inside Western Europe and inside the Atlantic alliance, but still perceive NATO discipline and West European political integration as inevitable and to a degree useful to its purposes. Although they would be contradictory if pushed to their ultimate conclusion, the various facets of Soviet policy are not mutually exclusive, and the balance between them can be modified as circumstances require.[33] In accordance with Gorbachev's policy style, acceptance of greater unity in the West has been expressed as part of a new vision of interdependence and in the context of a positive campaign for rapprochement, in which the European Community is invited to play a part in forwarding continent-wide European cooperation rather than blocking it.[34]

What calculation of costs, benefits, dangers and opportunities lies behind this change?

(c) The approach to Western Europe

Economic relations
In the course of the 1980s the urgency for the USSR and its allies of preserving and widening trade links with Western Europe and access to its resources of technological and managerial expertise has increased. While signs of economic recovery emerged in the West, growth rates continued to fall in Eastern-bloc countries. Talk of 'crisis' became more common. Meanwhile, as specialists in Moscow continued to put the case for exploiting the benefits of international specialization, the Soviet leaders could observe that from 1984 trade with Western Europe (four-fifths of all Soviet trade with the West) was in absolute decline. Repeated attempts to alter its composition – exporting more manufactures and fewer energy goods and raw materials – had failed. As two economists wrote in 1987, time was running out for the USSR 'to occupy a place in the world division of labour more appropriate to its economic, scientific and technological potential'.[35]

Apart from geographical proximity and the relative weight of Western Europe in existing CMEA foreign trade, there were a number of reasons why the region should be selected as the principal focus for the USSR's efforts to expand its foreign economic ties. There were complementarities between the Soviet (and to some extent the East European) and West European economies in labour costs, skills, specialized production, raw materials, and so on. The United States was relatively more self-sufficient. In any case, the experience of trade negotiations with the Americans in the 1970s had been unhappy, with a whole series of instances of political disruption. The 1982 gas pipeline dispute had shown that West European leaders were prepared to incur political costs in Washington in order to avoid losing Soviet contracts. Their commercial and political interests in maintaining East-West European economic contacts were perceived as strong and mutually reinforcing.

What expectations there may have been of a 'Gaullist' evolution of Western Europe, accompanied by a relatively rapid decline of American hegemony, faded in the mid-1980s, but even a somewhat more dependent, economically weaker Western Europe was an attractive partner for trade and cooperation. The predominant and immediate need, after all, was not for the most advanced world technology, but for the hardware and know-how to revitalize already-established sectors, especially engineering. The region could serve as an access route to the ever more closely integrated world economy. Its competitive weaknesses were indeed envisaged by some writers as a factor which might encourage it to pool its efforts with those of the CMEA countries.[36]

The USSR is interested in freer credits and lower tariff barriers mainly for the sake of its CMEA partners. As reports from Brussels in 1987 indicated, its own first priority is to establish favourable conditions for cooperation in research and development, at a time when Western Europe's technology policy is at a formative stage. As we have seen, specialists were being consulted, and concrete proposals were emerging for East-West links in areas such as thermonuclear synthesis, production applications of new technology, space research, environmental protection, communications and transport, for participation in Eureka, partnership with agencies like the European Space Agency (ESA) and the European Centre for Nuclear Research (CERN), and joint ventures in advanced technology sectors.[37]

Even the most sceptical Soviet commentators acknowledged the advances which Western Europe had made towards creating effective political machinery for devising and monitoring cooperative programmes. They suggested that the accumulated experience and skills in economic integration could be exploited on a wider, continental scale, building on existing inter-system links. Despite formal non-recognition of the EC, East Germany already had privileged access to the Common Market, while limited bilateral agreements had been signed by Brussels and various East European states. A number of circumstances argued for prompt action. Spain, Portugal and Greece looked likely to be followed by other applicants for membership in, or closer association with, the Community. With the plans for introducing a single market by 1992, the USSR and the other CMEA countries faced the same danger of 'missing the boat' (as one Soviet writer put it), as the EC's other major partners did. The tightening-up of COCOM export restrictions seemed to indicate that they could suffer even more harshly. The IMEMO journal wrote:

The EC now includes the majority of West European states. The EFTA member countries are being drawn more and more into collaboration with them, which also solidifies Western Europe around the Community. However, the formation of a single West European market separates the Eastern and Western parts of the continent. Recently, moreover, the socialist countries have been completely excluded from the Community's technology market.[38]

Eastern Europe

The fear that a prosperous and united Western Europe would act as a disintegrating influence on the Eastern bloc was undoubtedly one of the principal reasons why Moscow refused for thirty years to recognize the European Community. The USSR has every reason to be apprehensive, since its own control over its allies has often appeared to rest fundamentally on armed force.[39] The political fragility of its alliance means that its recent change of policy must have required difficult decisions.

Soviet commentators over the decades have complained about the West's deliberate 'bridge-building' to the East, and about its declared strategy of splitting the CMEA countries by distributing trading and other concessions on a differentiated basis. Even in the mid-1980s, achieving an agreement between the CMEA and the European Community was explicitly described in Soviet sources as a means of hampering politically motivated, 'subversive' discrimination, and when negotiations were reopened Soviet writers initially greeted it as a sign that Brussels was preparing to revise its previous insistence on having the right to deal with individual CMEA members.[40] As it turned out, Moscow instead effectively accepted the Commission's previous conditions, and has persisted with its more forthcoming policy in the face of unequivocal statements from Brussels to the effect that the EC intends to exploit the new opportunities for encouraging market-oriented economic reform and human rights concessions by offering specially favourable terms to particular countries.[41] Hungary, the most obvious target for this kind of pressure, had been permitted by Moscow to approach the Community with proposals for a trade agreement as early as 1984. The document was initialled at the end of June 1988, a week after the signing of the EC-CMEA declaration. Meanwhile talks about renewing the existing agreement with Romania were demonstratively placed on the back burner.[42]

This volte-face reflected the greater sense of urgency about coming to terms with the European Community which has already been referred to, and in addition a new, less fearful conception of the relationship between detente and bloc cohesion, in the East as in the West. There are signs that the Soviet leadership is moving towards an understanding in relation to its own allies, writes one Western advocate of closer trans-European links, that 'no amount of superficial uniformity in external bloc relations will produce cohesion if it does not already exist on a more substantial basis; conversely, if an alliance enjoys real cohesion based on the unified pursuit of core systemic goals, diverse external actions can be taken without undermining that cohesion.'[43]

In accordance with the general political decompression under Gorbachev, a new doctrine of non-interference in the affairs of other socialist states has gradually emerged in Moscow. In 1984, when superpower relations were at a low ebb, the East German and Hungarian leaderships argued in vain for the smaller European states to be allowed to play a special part in reviving detente. After some hesitation, the Soviet Union rejected this initiative, unloosing a campaign for bloc solidarity and against German revanchism. After Gorbachev came to power the Central Committee officials responsible for this decision (Rusakov, Rakhmanin) were replaced, and second-rank figures such as Zagladin and Bovin, who had cautiously indicated support for Berlin and Budapest, came to the fore. The men who were put in charge of Moscow's bloc relations, Medvedev and Shakhnazarov, clearly held quite a different view from their predecessors of how the USSR should strike the balance between maintaining control in Eastern Europe and allowing the local regimes to find their own path to building popular support.[44] Inter-German diplomacy flourished, and Honecker's long-delayed visit to the Federal Republic took place in September 1987. 'The days of Comintern and Cominform and even the days of binding international conferences are over,' declared the Soviet General Secretary two months later, and more or less explicitly apologized for his country's earlier interventions in the affairs of the Warsaw Pact allies.[45]

Embracing so wholeheartedly a programme of greater diversity and flexibility inside the Eastern bloc, the Soviet leaders were again

71

to some extent making a virtue of necessity. They no doubt calculated that (1) after a decade and a half of Ostpolitik, and the achievements of the Helsinki process, the West European threat was apparently no longer one of immediate subversion; (2) the old arguments for monolithic solidarity could no longer be sustained in a renewed atmosphere of detente; (3) greater freedom of initiative would allow their allies to solve their (many) internal problems more effectively; (4) a 'hands-off' policy in Eastern Europe would lessen apprehensions in the Western part of the continent; and (5) pan-European cooperation might be encouraged by allowing greater political and economic variety in Eastern Europe to blur the boundaries between the two systems.

Thus, instead of perceiving a simple trade-off between defending gains in Eastern Europe or better exploiting relations with Western Europe, Moscow appears to have taken the view that it can make its East and West European policies reinforce each other and pull in the same direction. It was therefore able to swim with the tide of increasing 'all-European' sentiment in both halves of the continent. In this respect Gorbachev's speeches in Prague and Warsaw in favour of transcontinental cooperation were clearly aimed as much at his local audiences as they were at his foreign ones. There are no grounds to suppose, on the other hand, that the Soviet Union's determination to preserve the Warsaw Pact structure is in any way diminished, or that the peoples of Eastern Europe have become any more reconciled to their enforced membership of the organization. The underlying dilemmas remain, and continue to pose problems for policy-makers in both Eastern and Western Europe. They will be discussed at length in the next chapter.

Military relations

It has frequently been argued that Moscow pursues a policy of military pressure and blackmail in Europe. 'If the Soviet Union can convincingly demonstrate that NATO has no viable defensive option in Western Europe,' wrote one specialist in 1984, 'a process of political accommodation is likely to set in.' Its arms build-up, its arms control policy and its support for the anti-war movement appear in this version of events as components of a single coherent strategy.[46] The evidence of Chapter 4 is that such a strategy is no longer perceived as viable. Security, it is now officially declared, can be achieved only on the condition that neither side feels threatened.

The deployment of SS-20s has been criticized in the Soviet press, and the missiles are being removed.[47] The utility of the Warsaw Pact's superiority in battle tanks has been openly questioned, and serious offers of negotiation and unilateral concessions are being made in the conventional arms sphere.[48] Comments in the specialist press about the depth of West European apprehension and mistrust of the USSR have been echoed by authoritative journalists and by the General Secretary himself.[49]

Since Reykjavik, as we have seen, awareness has also been growing that excessive haste and neglect of all-round consultation in disarmament matters can be perceived in the West as unwelcome pressure, and provoke unforeseen reactions. Official Soviet statements occasionally express incomprehension about the motives for 'compensation' proposals for deploying new weapons following on the INF agreement, and projects for military cooperation in Western Europe. In less public forums, however, Foreign Ministry employees were prepared to take some of the blame on themselves:

> Occasionally we fail in trying to reach the other bank to indicate clearly enough the bridges leading to it, which causes scepticism among some of our pragmatic Western partners. Also, we must adduce more detailed arguments taking account of West European conditions.[50]

For years Soviet journalists have been writing articles with titles like 'Europe at the Crossroads'. But by the second half of the 1980s an important turning-point really was approaching. The agreement on dismantling land-based intermediate-range nuclear missiles focused attention on the growing importance of conventional arms in strategic thinking on both sides, and on the question of how long the United States would be willing to act as the principal guardian of Western Europe's security. Even without any radical changes, a new high-technology arms race was under way, and the arguments for closer defence collaboration in Europe were being heard more and more frequently. Choices had to be made. Most immediately, what was to be done about asymmetries in the conventional force balance which the trend to nuclear disarmament was throwing into relief? In the longer term, how far were the West European powers intending to rely on enhanced nuclear deterrence and/or a large-scale conventional arms build-up, on a cooperative or even integrated basis, and how far would they contemplate making agreements with the Warsaw Pact for substantial reductions in arms and manpower?

The answers to these questions were important for the Soviet Union not just in relation to expenditure levels and challenges to its military-technological resources, expensive as the outcome might be; they were also crucial for Gorbachev's overall foreign policy strategy, which strove to lower the temperature of political confrontation. It is unlikely, for instance, that Western governments could muster the domestic backing for the huge increases in spending which would be required to mount a more Europe-based defence effort, in the absence of a level of international tension comparable with that which marked NATO's early years. For Moscow, the prospect of a third Cold War – with Europe acting as the focus of conflict rather than as a force for conciliation – is something to be avoided at almost any cost.

Exploiting divisions in Western Europe: the German case
Even if Moscow is more aware of the underlying cohesiveness of NATO, and has taken a decision to work with the grain of trends to greater West European unity, this does not mean that it has forsworn the practice of exploiting differences of opinion in the West. Indeed Gorbachev's stated preference for political rather than military means in international relations implies a much more active manipulation of actual or potential rifts. The USSR values closer foreign policy cooperation among the European allies principally because this diminishes the likelihood of the United States having everything its own way. It continues to promote the Helsinki process as a means of mobilizing 'all-European consciousness' and bringing into play the preferences of the smaller NATO powers and the European neutrals.

The USSR has played quite blatantly on allied disagreements over strategic issues, most obviously between Paris, London and Washington in the case of SDI, but also between Bonn and its European partners over the future of short-range nuclear weapons.[51] In a similar way, the shift in emphasis from aggressive support for public peace campaigns (against the neutron bomb, SDI, cruise and Pershing-II deployment) to state-to-state diplomacy has in no way meant neglecting the task of winning over wider public opinion.[52] As we have seen, specialists who sympathize with Gorbachev's new thinking frequently comment on how the new Soviet image in the

West is putting electoral pressure on governments to take up a more moderate posture.

The recent course of Soviet/West German relations provides good illustrations of these dimensions of leverage politics. The Federal Republic occupies a crucial place in NATO in a military and a political sense, and it is the economic pivot of Europe as a whole. It is also, in Edwina Moreton's words, 'uniquely vulnerable to Soviet pressure and encouragement'.[53] It has easily exploitable interests in freer conditions for East-West trade and technical assistance and in risk-reduction (and now denuclearization) on the central NATO front.

During Gorbachev's first years in power it was a question more of pressure than of encouragement. As we have seen, there has always been apprehension in Moscow about West Germany's intentions in the military sphere, and about the impact of its influence on the German Democratic Republic and the rest of Eastern Europe. During the period from 1984 to 1986 the ruling coalition in Bonn vigorously supported cruise and Pershing-II deployment, and it was closely involved in NATO's conventional force modernization projects. There were suspicions in Moscow that West Germany had plans to use its economic power in order to change the map of Eastern Europe. All this led the USSR to subject Bonn to a prolonged spell of diplomatic isolation. Warnings about the dangers of German 'militarism and revanchism' were broadcast all over the continent. The spectre was raised of the Federal Republic acquiring nuclear weapons through participation in West European defence cooperation projects, and it was accused of making plans to spread subversion among its Eastern neighbours. The threat to peace, Aleksandr Yakovlev warned those of Moscow's own allies who might be tempted by German overtures, was 'perfectly obvious even to the least objective observer'.[54]

At this time the Federal government received scarcely any of the public attention which was lavished on its European allies, and for that matter on its own opposition. The SPD was treated with what Wettig describes as 'ostentatious cordiality'. It was drawn into cooperation on joint projects: it worked together with the SED on plans for nuclear- and chemical-free zones in Europe, and with the Polish United Workers' Party it backed a proposal to create a European Confidence-Building Council. From 1984 to 1987 a joint CPSU-SPD working party met regularly to work out plans for redirecting funds from military budgets to Third World development.[55]

In 1986 and 1987 the Soviet Union relaxed and simplified somewhat its foreign trade procedures, and held out the prospect of large engineering equipment contracts and joint ventures. By the autumn of 1987 a thaw in Moscow-Bonn relations was at last under way. West Germany argued inside the Western alliance for reducing restrictions on trade and mounting a major drive to build economic interdependence in Europe as a whole. Simultaneously the Federal Republic was induced to move from supporting cruise and Pershing-II deployment to embracing the goal of removing all theatre nuclear forces, and began to make objections to plans for nuclear weapons modernization.[56] In April 1988 Egon Bahr was reported in *Izvestiya* as saying that the ruling parties and the opposition in Bonn shared an identical position on disarmament issues.[57]

In 1987 several Soviet officials dropped hints about ill-specified relaxations in the inter-German relationship. On German television on 1 October, for example, Valentin Falin stated that the Four-Power Agreement on Berlin was not necessarily 'the final word' on the status of the city, and other more far-reaching proposals were rumoured at about the same time.[58] This could be interpreted as a way of tempting the West Germans by raising the prospect of moves in the direction of reunification, but such a view seems unjustified in the light of the repeatedly and forcefully stated Soviet position that the German question is 'closed' for the foreseeable future. It is noticeable that spokesmen such as Aleksandr Bovin, who advocated a freer hand for Honecker in inter-German diplomacy in 1984, have kept closely to the official line. Perhaps the main function of the kite-flying by Falin and others is to remind the East German leadership of its dependence on the Soviet Union.[59]

Clearly, the underlying dilemma for Moscow of how to bring about wider political and economic contacts between the two halves of Europe, without seeing its sphere of influence and its security interests eroded, and the East European states drawn into a Western orbit, would be enormously aggravated if any kind of closer relationship were to emerge between the Federal Republic and the GDR which threatened the latter's identity and autonomy. The Soviet Union thus has every incentive to back up Honecker's position that joining the German states together would be like trying to combine 'fire and water'.[60] In any case, as time goes by and generations pass, reunification may decline in relative importance among the various other powerful incentives for West Germany to pursue a more active Eastern policy.

All this does not mean that a return to Soviet-German diplomacy on the interwar pattern is on the agenda. All the evidence of the specialist literature and the official statements summarized in the preceding pages confirms that the Federal Republic is now perceived to be attached by thousands of threads to the wider Western world.

* * *

When one looks at the evolution of Soviet policy over the last half-decade, it is clear that there has been an important shift in attitude towards Western Europe since the end of the Brezhnev era. At that time Adam Ulam spoke for many of his colleagues when he declared that preventing West European unity 'must remain the cardinal objective of Kremlin politics'.[61] That is no longer a convincing view. This change has been part of a wider adjustment. In 1984 one Western writer listed six key Soviet aims in relation to the Atlantic alliance: (1) to win recognition of the territorial and systemic status quo; (2) to protect Eastern Europe and the USSR against Western interference; (3) to retain and broaden access to Western technology, know-how and credits; (4) to limit political cooperation in the EC and NATO; (5) to deny Western Europe any viable defensive option and make it aware of its vulnerability; and (6) to encourage radical internal change with the help of communist and other 'peace-loving' forces.[62] While the first of these remains important, and the third has become even more pressing, it is plain that the remaining four have been sharply downgraded, and are regarded as less urgent, less realistic or, in the case of the fifth and sixth, probably even so counterproductive that they should be abandoned altogether. What the consequences of the new approach are likely to be is the topic of the final chapter.

6

PROSPECTS FOR A 'COMMON EUROPEAN HOME'

At the end of the 1980s deep-running changes are in progress in both Eastern and Western Europe, and there are numerous sources of uncertainty about the future of the continent. As far as the USSR is concerned, the outcome of the internal political struggle is still in doubt. It is obvious that there has been a radical shift in foreign policy, but the outlines of Soviet intentions in Europe are still not clear. As we have seen, many key issues in this area are still a source of disagreement among specialists in Moscow. No doubt they also provoke argument among decision-makers. This chapter will begin with some comments about the likely impact on foreign policy of Soviet domestic politics, and the ambiguities in Moscow's approach to Europe. It will then take a broader perspective, and look at the possible impact of international political factors.

Internal politics
At first glance it is tempting to interpret Gorbachev's new, more cooperative approach to Western Europe and the Western alliance as part of a cyclical pattern in which the failure of an aggressively 'trouble-making' strategy forces the Soviet leadership to adopt a conciliatory posture, biding its time until detente brings round more favourable conditions for activism. But there are longer-term factors at work. The version of the revolution in Soviet foreign-policy thinking advanced at the beginning of the preceding chapter implies that a protracted learning process, involving the shedding of illusions about Western weakness and Soviet strength, has finally

worked its way through the system. During the latest phase, members of the foreign policy establishment have left their posts in large numbers, the agencies which compose it have undergone a sharp readjustment of relative status and representation, and there has been unprecedented public criticism of previous policy.

The passing of generations and the shedding of illusions imply a degree of irreversibility, particularly if they are seen in the context of a delayed 'modernization' of Soviet society, which favours the Western-oriented intelligentsia at the expense of older-established elites.[1] On the doctrinal level the political upheaval is reflected in iconoclastic revisionism. The theory of class conflict in international relations, for example, which ostensibly expressed Party militancy but in effect served as a justification for coercive solutions to national security problems (as in 1956, 1968 and 1979), has been publicly criticized as a typical post-revolutionary misconception, which persisted beyond its time because of intellectual inertia and dogmatism.[2]

If Gorbachev were to be unseated in the near future, or a substantial change were to take place in the political balance of the Soviet leadership, it is unlikely that foreign policy would be subject to radical alteration. There is too widespread and too fresh an awareness of the costs of unrestrained East-West rivalry, and of the urgent need for wider economic collaboration with the OECD countries, even if only to maintain current living standards and sustain a minimal competitive capability.

Yet the West's caution is understandable. The perception of Soviet threat has been so long-standing, and the emergence of the new thinking apparently so sudden, that groups and individuals opposed to any 'lowering of NATO's guard' can argue persuasively for a wait-and-see policy. Because Gorbachev himself has been so closely associated with the innovations in Soviet conduct and doctrine, any internal difficulties which he experiences can easily seem to cast a shadow over the future of Moscow's relations with the West. This undermines the Soviet leaders' current strategy of using successes abroad to compensate for slower progress in less tractable spheres of reform, such as the economy.

The 'Common European Home': problems of definition
There are problems for the Soviet Union in combining its European policy with its broader approach to the West. Its main goal is to

reach agreements with Washington and the alliance as a whole. As earlier chapters have shown, this is the only strategy which is now perceived as viable in view of the underlying cohesiveness of the Atlantic community and persisting West European fears of the USSR, and it is the one which has been determinedly followed by Gorbachev and his fellow leaders. At the same time Moscow builds bridges specifically to West European states. This is done, first, in order to exploit the opportunities for profitable collaboration offered by geography and a long-established network of contacts; and, second, in order to manipulate the levers of intra-NATO politics, for example by playing on pro-detente attitudes on the continent.

Both these motives, we know, are openly discussed in the Soviet specialist press. We know that Soviet foreign affairs experts write much more openly than before about the limitations of the second, political, approach, and that in practice it is employed less crudely than before, in a way calculated to produce East-West agreements. Yet the impression persists from the days of earlier Soviet all-European campaigning that the 'European Home' is essentially a device for shutting out the United States. The phrase was first used by Brezhnev on a visit to Bonn in 1981, and the apparent continuity between his and Gorbachev's European policies was underlined by the militantly anti-American sections of the 27th Party Congress Report in 1986, by explicit statements in the Soviet press that Europe was 'somebody else's house' as far as Washington was concerned, and by the kind of specialist analysis reviewed above which spelt out the USA's interests in opposing East-West European rapprochement.[3] The obverse of the image of Europe as a continent of political maturity, cooperativeness and high civilization was a picture of the United States as a danger to world peace and of American culture as a source of materialism and violence. The appeal to common European values, moreover, has a contrived quality in view of the profound cultural affinities which bind the nations on each side of the Atlantic, and in view of the way in which the Soviet Union cut itself off for so long from contacts with its Western neighbours, imposing a set of values which were apprehended by most West Europeans as profoundly alien.

The occasional exclusive, anti-American flavour in Soviet Common European Home rhetoric is particularly alarming, even to 'Europeanist' Europeans, when it is seen in the context of plans for radical changes in strategic arrangements, for example denuclearization and large-scale troop withdrawals. In a common home stretching from the Atlantic to the Urals, the Soviet Union would simply occupy too high a proportion of the floor space for the psychological comfort of its fellow inhabitants. Many share Pierre Hassner's perception of the USSR as 'an objective Finlandizer' in relation to a Western Europe not closely tied to the United States, simply by virtue of its proximity, its size and its military capability.[4]

In the second half of the 1980s, after Soviet foreign affairs writers had begun to write more realistically about West European security concerns, and in particular about fears of decoupling, adjustments were made to the specification of the Common European Home:

The meaning of the concept of the European home has nothing to do with the creation of a united Europe as opposed to the USA, or isolated from the USA. For most Americans, too, Europe is the common home of their ancestors, and it is there in the Old World that their historical and spiritual roots lie. Can one, in general, speak of Europe outside the framework of intensive ties with North America? We would welcome the Americans' participation in the construction of the European home.[5]

Soviet writers also took pains to emphasize that the new vision of Europe has nothing to do with traditional geopolitical categories, but rests on an understanding of common interests, interdependence and all-human values.[6]

Yet jarring notes could still be heard. At the end of 1987 Valentin Falin was still claiming that 'the cult of power' which permeated American society made it difficult for Washington even to conceive of what a less confrontational relationship with the USSR in Europe would be like. At the beginning of 1989, in his closing address to the CSCE delegates in Vienna, Shevardnadze himself called for more attention to be given to what he termed 'cultural ecology', declaring that it was immoral when 'ruthless laws of economic competition spread to the spiritual sphere, when cultural expansion backed by advanced technology and capital implants alien values and standards in Europe and elsewhere'.[7]

Thus Soviet spokesmen still reproduce in their statements about the Common European Home the fundamental conflict in perceptions of European-American relations which was identified above. On one side is a 'strong Europeanism' which takes an optimistic view of the potential for encouraging political autonomy from the United States of a kind which would serve Soviet purposes. On the other is an increasingly dominant, but by no means universal, 'moderate Europeanism' which sees more clearly the strength and depth of Atlantic ties, especially in matters of defence.

The renewed vigour of the Common European Home campaign in the late 1980s should not be interpreted, of course, as a symptom of a swing-back to anti-American Europeanism in Moscow. It reflects, rather, the increased awareness of the European Community's continued momentum towards greater political, economic and military unity. This has created a feeling of urgency in the Soviet Union about the need to avoid decisions being taken which will raise new barriers on the continent and create new foci of tension between East and West. It is fuelled, too, by a more lively sense of the importance of reaching understandings with the major West European states on security issues. This is stimulated by, and has helped to accelerate, progress towards conventional arms reduction agreements.

The outline of the 'common home' vision is blurred not only by the variety of the purposes it is intended to serve, but also by the diversity of the publics which it is designed to appeal to. It is aimed at 'Europeanists' of left and right in the West, who may be interested in ways of increasing their freedom of manoeuvre vis-à-vis the United States. It is aimed at those who are interested mainly in expanding profitable commercial contacts with their Eastern neighbours. It is aimed at those who wish to take a few more steps on the long road which leads to German reunification. In Eastern Europe and the USSR it promises to Western-oriented intellectuals a lifting of the barriers to communication and travel that were lowered during the Stalin era, and the possibility of a social-democratic evolution of their political regime. To those engaged in economic management it offers a realistic strategy for modernization through easier access to the appropriate markets.

Because the concept is so ill-defined, the slogan of the Common European Home is less useful than it might be in East-West European communications, and in certain respects positively harmful. Soviet Deputy Foreign Minister Petrovsky was at the very least exaggerating when he declared in February 1988 that the idea 'is becoming essentially very acceptable to all European states'. More to the point was Margarita Maksimova's statement, published later in the same year:

> The main thing is that there still does not exist a sufficiently clear scholarly conception of the 'Common European Home', nor is there available a constructive programme of actions to implement the idea. Many questions remain to be answered. For example, what must the level of security be on the continent? What part will be played in the 'Common European Home' by the United States of America? How will the Single European Market of the European Community and the planned common market of the CMEA countries 'engage with' each other in the future? What institutions and machinery will be used to control and direct the building of the 'Common European Home'? And so on.[8]

Maksimova's questions draw attention to serious potential obstacles in the path of Moscow's European policy. There are problems which in many cases will require much more far-reaching discussion than they have so far received, at least in the published versions of Soviet specialist commentary. They can be broadly categorized as problems of East-West economic relations in Europe, problems of Eastern-bloc politics, and problems of Western alliance relations.

Problems of East-West European economic relations
There is sense in the Soviet contention that Europe represents a good testing ground for inter-bloc regional economic cooperation because of the accumulated expertise in matters of integration and the existing network of trans-European links.[9] The Soviet Union has taken sizeable steps towards overcoming some long-standing obstacles to progress. It has abandoned its insistence on a CMEA common front, and has opened the door to bilateral deals between its allies and Brussels. It has begun to simplify its foreign trade procedures, demonstrating a readiness to open up to freer contacts with the West. It has sanctioned more far-reaching liberalization in parts of Eastern Europe.

Yet progress has been slow. The slump in trade with Western Europe (trade turnover with the Federal Republic of Germany was by 1987 at less than half its 1985 level) continued into 1988. Foreign businessmen were reluctant to invest in enterprises on Soviet soil on the terms which were being offered. The obstacles to improvement are frankly discussed in Moscow, but no means of removing them in the foreseeable future have been devised. Low world fuel prices and accumulated payments deficits in certain East European countries have only aggravated a situation which essentially arises from the inability of the CMEA states to export manufactured goods of competitive quality. Barriers imposed by the West, in the form of trade embargoes and credit restrictions, and bureaucratic red tape in the East (what Soviet writers call 'our internal COCOM') are going to be difficult to remove. Slimming down the COCOM list is a vexed issue among the NATO states, and a radical reduction of tariffs set by the EC's Common Agricultural Policy looks unlikely.

Gorbachev's *perestroika* should in theory solve those problems which arise on the Soviet side. Yet it is readily admitted that reforms in the foreign trade sphere are not having the desired effect, partly because of lack of progress in the restructuring of the internal economy, and there is little confidence of early successes in that area. In the CMEA as a whole, different countries are taking such diverse approaches to economic reform that the process seems likely to create more problems in intra-bloc trade and cooperation than it solves. Different economies will adopt varying degrees of decentralization of management, varying price policies and varying attitudes to the timetable for achieving currency convertibility. The consequent disarray will put the East at even more of a disadvantage in negotiations with the European Community states, whose economies seem set to become more closely integrated. The Community is not only a much more competitive trading bloc than the CMEA, it is also much more closely linked to the world market. EC-CMEA trade in 1986 amounted to 3 per cent of EC member states' exports and 14 per cent of CMEA members' exports. Some 85 per cent of CMEA trade with the advanced capitalist economies is with the European Community. Underlying all this is the gap in levels of development, which means that policy-makers in the Eastern-bloc countries may well frequently perceive a choice between strict regulation of external links on the one hand and dependency on the other.[10]

In a situation such as this a great deal depends on Western governments adopting a constructive attitude, on whether they are prepared to take a long view and, as one of their spokesmen has put it, promote change without precipitating chaos in Eastern Europe.[11] The USSR is in an unenviably vulnerable position. The problem of creating an acceptable system of East-West trade in Europe is only one aspect of the wider puzzle for Moscow of how its relations with its allies might be shaped in an era of East-West European rapprochement.

Problems of Eastern-bloc politics

Some idea of the issues which will have to be weighed by the Soviet leadership as the East European states begin to form closer ties to the European Community emerged in the second half of 1988, when the subject of Austrian entry to the Common Market came to the fore. The initial reaction in Moscow was far less hostile than would have been thought possible five years earlier. In September Shevardnadze stated publicly that he understood Austria's desire to find a means of ensuring access to the Single European Market. At the same time he expressed disquiet about it entering a grouping in which almost all the participants were NATO members, and 'where processes of integration in the sphere of foreign policy, including its military aspects, were gathering ever greater strength'. On his return from a visit to Moscow shortly after this, the Austrian Chancellor, Franz Vranitzky, reported that the Soviet leadership seemed to be inclining to the view that EC membership and neutrality might after all be compatible in the case of his country.[12] However much wishful thinking there may have been in this account, the fact that it could even be considered credible indicated the seriousness of the turnaround in Soviet strategy, from one of defensive barrier-raising to one of building bridges, of 'overcoming the East-West divide in Europe'. Yet the fundamental problems have not gone away. In his own talks with Vranitzky, the Soviet President singled out what he called Austria's active and constructive role in the European process. Turning to the European Community's plans for a Single Market, he commented:

> It was perfectly obvious that economic integration was an objective process. It was also obvious that economic ties preceded political interaction ... Combining economic internationalization with political independence was a great problem. On the other hand, what would be the future of the all-European

process if the Western part of Europe locked itself up within the rigid framework of the new formation? How would it be possible to build a 'European home'?[13]

In a series of loosely connected remarks, Gorbachev went on to identify a similar contradiction between 'the existence of East and West Europe', and 'the aspiration of all Europeans to move towards one another'. These reflections point to a fundamental tension in the USSR's European policy. It must balance the opportunities offered by interaction with the more advanced states to the West against the threat that such interaction poses to its control over its allies. Moscow's fears on this score, as well as alarm about the role being played by Bonn in NATO defence debates, undoubtedly lay behind the violent denunciations of West German 'revanchism' which were published in 1984 and 1985.

This Western 'threat' to the East does not seem likely to diminish in the foreseeable future. The gap in technology, productivity and living standards continues to widen. As the European Community becomes more united and absorbs – or draws into a closer relationship – its EFTA neighbours, so the gravitational pull on the East European states with which it is now free to conclude bilateral agreements is bound to increase. The Commission has made no secret of its intention of pursuing a differentiated approach to the CMEA states for its own political ends. As Soviet foreign affairs writers have remarked, West German Europeanism is beginning to acquire a more pan-European colouring, but 'they have their own concept', and it does not entirely coincide with the Soviet one.[14]

Meanwhile the individual socialist states are faced with uncomfortable choices. The traditional economic and political model has been discredited, but experience has shown that attempts to change it put social stability at risk. Political reform in Eastern Europe can be characterized by the words used by a Soviet conservative to describe attempts at democratization in his own country, when he likened it to 'an aeroplane which is taking off without anyone knowing where it is going to land'. Among the most destabilizing effects is likely to be the release of nationalist tendencies. These are capable of giving rise to a combination of internal upheavals, conflicts between East European states (as between Hungary and

Romania in 1988), and, more seriously, moves to break free from the socialist community altogether.

Gorbachev's deliberate relaxing of bloc discipline cannot but increase the uncertainty. As in Soviet domestic politics, he is gambling that a transition – from relations based on coercion to relations based on authority, consent and responsibility – can be made without revolution. This act of faith may prove to be unjustified. It is true that the CMEA states, with their less-developed economies, share common interests opposed to those of their more prosperous neighbours. It is also the case that the communist leaders have interests in preserving the structures and relationships which underpin their hold on power. But the West has ample resources at its disposal with which it could, if it wished, tempt particular countries to break ranks, and changes in the internal political climate might well make it difficult for governments to ignore popular aspirations.

It remains to be seen whether the motives for solidarity are sufficiently strong, and whether there is a clear enough perception in East European capitals of what the boundaries of the permissible are in Soviet eyes. In Karen Dawisha's judgment, the USSR's allies are well aware that the road ahead lies through gradual change within the limits of 'socialism' and compatible with Warsaw Pact viability.[15] But in an atmosphere of 'Europeanism', detente, doctrinal revision-ism and flux in military thinking, it is easy to see how miscalcula-tions could be made. If a situation developed which led to Soviet military intervention, say in East Germany or Poland, the delicate transition from Cold War logic to the logic of interdependence would be thrown violently into reverse.

For this reason the immediate Soviet priority in Eastern Europe is probably to preserve maximum continuity and stability consonant with the continued viability of the regimes there until internal transformations in the USSR and the restructuring of East-West relations are on a firmer footing. Soviet policy-makers are no doubt fully aware of the dilemmas facing the USSR's allies and of the hazards of uncontrolled change, and are therefore not too displeased with the conservative course being followed by states such as Czechoslovakia and East Germany. The latter in particular would find it difficult to make many liberalizing changes without losing the justification for its separateness from, say, a social-democratic

Federal Republic. Yet in so far as such states participate in the general increased tendency of East European countries to follow a more independent line in internal and external policy, they contribute to the general unpredictability.

Alliance problems

The USSR's current strategy is unprecedentedly difficult for the NATO states to resist. It combines genuine domestic reform, radical changes in ideology, active appeals to Western public opinion, and disarmament proposals which often echo those made by Western goverments and which are designed to be taken seriously. It becomes more and more difficult to justify increasing expenditure on defence to taxpayers, in the face of a less and less threatening threat. This comes at a time when the United States is again pressing for a more even sharing-out of the cost burden, and when strategic thinking is emphasizing the importance of expensive new conventional arms.[16]

Gorbachev cannot be confident, however, that this policy will bring quick results. For one thing, there is a quite natural scepticism in the face of such a sudden transformation in the Soviet posture, coupled with suspicious elements of continuity with previous policies. Warsaw Pact proposals for collective security in Europe date back, after all, to its founding treaty document (Article 11). During the 1970s Moscow loudly advocated peace and disarmament on the continent at the same time as it built up its conventional forces and improved its capability to forward an offensive strategy in the European theatre.

Such mistrust can be overcome with time and persistence, of course, and it has tended to ebb away over recent years. Complications are also introduced, however, by cross-currents inside the NATO alliance. Separate steps taken to lower the level of confrontation may affect the interests of particular member states in special ways, sparking off anxieties about the decoupling of the United States from Europe's defence, for example, or about trends to neutralism in West Germany.[17] With the best will in the world, it is a task of the greatest delicacy for NATO to devise a concerted plan for arms reductions and withdrawals. Things are not made easier by the changes which are under way in military technology and doctrine.

Stability and a high level of coordination in the Western alliance are necessary if substantial constructive changes are to take place in the East-West strategic relationship in Europe. Yet substantial changes of that kind are bound to shake up the alliance and make coordination more difficult. In the East, change threatens the cohesion of the Warsaw Pact, in different ways, at a time when any large-scale upheaval would undoubtedly weaken Gorbachev's own position and put his programme in jeopardy. Matters are complicated by the underlying long-term trend to the decline of superpower dominance inside the two blocs. The United States is keen to reduce its share of NATO costs. The current Soviet administration, meanwhile, has wagered its credibility on an undertaking to maintain the degree of control over its allies perceived as necessary for national security without returning to the coercive methods of the past.

If Soviet plans for Europe are to get anywhere, a great deal of untrodden territory will have to be traversed; as Maksimova has warned publicly, and others no doubt have commented in private, there is a shortage of maps and itineraries, and little is being done in the way of planning. Soviet specialist commentary on international affairs has tended to approach topics such as intra-alliance relations and all-European collaboration in a politicized style. Either it is argued, in 'centrifugalist' mode, that events will be shaped mainly by conflict and shifts in the balance of power, or an optimistic 'internationalist' view is presented of the potential for international cooperation. Now that conditions in Soviet social science have at last become more favourable to a less partisan and more critical approach, it is probable that more sustained analyses will emerge, which take balanced account of the opportunities and the obstacles to further rapprochement between East and West in Europe, although taboos will no doubt continue to surround the question of relations inside the Warsaw Pact.

As it is, the picture is an encouraging one in so far as it demonstrates how far Soviet experts (and implicitly policy-makers) have gone in freeing themselves from long-established stereotypes, coming to terms with unpalatable truths, and endorsing the principles of compromise and far-reaching mutual advantage in East-West negotiations. Both sides have to make sure that they achieve and sustain such a directness and freshness of understanding. The bigger challenge, however, is to devise ways of avoiding the pitfalls and blind alleys, and achieving the changes which are needed to build a safer and more cooperative Europe.

NOTES

In the footnotes the IMEMO journal *Mirovaya ekonomika i mezhdunarodnye otnosheniya* is abbreviated as *MEMO*. The USA Institute journal *SShA: ekonomika, politika, ideologiya* is abbreviated as *SShA*. The titles of articles in Soviet academic journals are not included here, but are given in a separate list at the end of the book. Translations, unless otherwise specified, are my own.

Chapter 1

 1 *Pravda*, 8 April 1985; Gorbachev's speech of 20 February 1985, cited in C. Schmidt-Häuer, *Gorbachev: The Path to Power* (London, Pan, 1986), p. 144. Cf. Gorbachev's references in December 1984 to the relative decline of American power and the rise of Western Europe and Japan (*Pravda*, 12 December 1984); and his Political Report to the 27th Congress of the CPSU (*Politicheskii doklad TsK KPSS XXVII S'ezdu Kommunisticheskoi Partii Sovetskogo Soyuza* [Moscow, Politizdat, 1986], p. 82): 'In world politics one cannot confine oneself to relations with any single, even a very important, country. As we know from experience, this only fosters the arrogance of power.'
 2 *Pravda*, 2 October 1985.
 3 The British Foreign Secretary did refer critically to SDI in his speeches to the RUSI in March 1985 and to the IISS in January 1987. The Soviet press's response to the first of these was particularly warm. *Pravda*, 15 April 1985. The second provoked accusations of 'mealy-mouthed evasion' from Richard Perle. *The Independent*, 3 February 1987. TASS's comments are cited in *The Guardian*, 6 January 1988.
 4 *Pravda*, 9 June 1988; *Pravda*, 17 July 1988. There were also regional

initiatives, such as the proposal for an 'Arctic peace zone' in Northern Europe, and 'zones' and 'corridors' in Central Europe. There were numerous proposals for talks and conferences, e.g. on military doctrine. See the statements issued by the Warsaw Pact in Budapest in June 1986, in Berlin in May 1987 and in Warsaw in June 1988.

5 J. Pinder, 'Integration in Western and Eastern Europe: Relations between the European Community and the CMEA', *Journal of Common Market Studies*, vol. 18, no. 2 (1979), pp. 114–34. Virtually all the East European states already had bilateral commercial agreements of one kind or another with the EC, despite the lack of formal sanction.

6 This proposal was preceded by discussions between Bruno Craxi and Gorbachev in May. *Le Monde*, 3 February 1986; *Le Monde*, 15/16 November 1987.

7 Foreign Broadcast Information Service, *Daily Report: Soviet Union* (Washington, DC), 16 October 1987.

8 *Soviet News*, 1 February 1989.

9 *Le Monde*, 29 March 1988.

10 *Soviet News*, 3 February 1988; *Pravda*, 30 March 1988; *Pravda*, 6 April 1988.

11 M. Gorbachev, *Perestroika* (London, Collins, 1987), pp. 197–8. The campaign for 'European' security arrangements dates back to the early postwar years. The 'European Home' concept was put forward by Brezhnev in Bonn in 1981. *Pravda*, 24 November 1981. A more recent pre-Gorbachev example is the remark made by V. Nekrasov, a member of the editorial board of *Kommunist*, in 1984: 'It is well-known that the history of the European peoples, be they on the east or west of the continent, is not subject to artificial division.' *Pravda*, 7 June 1984. Cited by J. Hough, 'Soviet Perspectives on European Security', *International Journal*, vol. 12 (1984–5), p. 38.

12 Gorbachev, *Perestroika*, pp. 196–7. Recent examples can be found in the report of Gorbachev's talks with Alessandro Natta in March 1988 (*Pravda*, 30 March 1988) and his speech to the Polish Sejm in July (*Pravda*, 12 July 1988).

13 *Perestroika*, pp. 208–9. See, too, Soviet reports of Gorbachev's talks with Lothar Späth and of Shevardnadze's with the British Foreign Secretary, both in *Soviet News*, 17 February 1988.

14 See, for instance, V. Lomeiko, *International Affairs* (Moscow), 1987, no. 12, pp. 104–5; also Gorbachev, *Perestroika*, p. 208.

15 *Politicheskii doklad*, p. 19.

16 Jerry Hough wrote of the emergence of an 'anti-American, pro-Europe, pro-Japan' faction in Soviet foreign policy making, supported by Yakovlev, Valentin Falin, and possibly Andropov, during 1983–4. 'Soviet Perspectives on European Security', pp. 40–1. See also

J. Hough, *The Struggle for the Third World* (Washington, DC, The
Brookings Institution, 1986), pp. 223–5; Martin Walker in *The
Guardian*, 25 November 1987: 'The Soviet Union has been quietly
reshaping its foreign policies to manage . . . the implications of American decline.' Aleksandr Yakovlev is now a full member of the Politburo with responsibilities in the foreign policy and ideological spheres.
He was First Deputy Head of the Propaganda Department of the
CPSU Central Commitee from 1965 to 1973, Ambassador to Canada
1973–83, Director of the Institute of the World Economy and International Relations 1983–5, Head of the CPSU Propaganda Department
from 1985, Candidate Member of the Politburo from February 1987,
full member from later in the same year, Chairman of the Central
Committee Commission on International Policy from 1988. Falin was
a senior Foreign Ministry official who managed the Soviet response to
Brandt's Ostpolitik. From the late 1970s until 1983 he was deputy
head of the CPSU International Information Department, from 1986
a Candidate Member of the Central Committee of the Party and head
of the Novosti press agency, from 1988 head of the Central Committee International Department.

17 P. Hassner, 'Europe between the United States and the Soviet Union',
Government and Opposition, vol. 21, no. 1, p. 30.

18 H. Adomeit, 'Capitalist Contradictions and Soviet Policy', *Problems
of Communism*, vol. 33, no. 3 (May-June 1984), p. 5. Cf. K. Pridham,
'The Soviet View of Current Disagreements between the United States
and Western Europe', *International Affairs* (London), vol. 59, no. 1
(1983), p. 17.

19 A clear and concise explanation of the traditional relationship
between theory and practice in Soviet foreign policy is given in M.
Light, *Soviet Theory of International Relations* (Brighton, Harvester-
Wheatsheaf, 1988), ch. 1, esp. p. 13.

20 During the 1970s there was a tendency in the West to overstate the
importance of the part played by academic specialists in Soviet foreign
policy making. They were undoubtedly overshadowed by other
civilian and military sources of advice and pressure. Now they are
undoubtedly better placed than before. F. Griffiths, 'Images, Politics
and Learning in Soviet Behavior towards the United States', doctoral
thesis, Columbia University, 1972, pp. 106–16; H. Adomeit, 'Soviet
Foreign Policy Making: The Internal Mechanism of Global Commit-
ment', in H. Adomeit, R. Boardman (eds.), *Foreign Policy Making in
Communist Countries* (New York, Praeger, 1979), p. 32; F. Griffiths,
'The Sources of American Conduct. Soviet Perspectives and their
Policy Implications', *International Security*, vol. 9, no. 2 (1984), pp. 3–
11; J. Hough, *The Struggle for the Third World*, pp. 13–36; M. Light,

Soviet Theory of International Relations, pp. 11–18; J. Snyder, 'The Gorbachev Revolution: A Waning of Soviet Expansionism', *International Security*, vol. 12, no. 3 (1987/8), pp. 93–131; N. Malcolm, 'Foreign Affairs Specialists and Decision Makers in the USSR', in D. Lane (ed.), *Elites and Political Power in the USSR* (London, Edward Elgar, 1988).

21 H. Adomeit, 'Soviet Perceptions of Western European Integration: Ideological Distortion or Realistic Assessment?' *Millennium*, vol. 8, no. 1 (1979), pp. 1–11; Adomeit, 'Capitalist Contradictions and Soviet Policy', pp. 3–4. Among other studies in English are C.A. Binns, 'From USE to EEC: the Soviet Analysis of European Integration under Capitalism', *Soviet Studies*, vol. 30, no. 2 (1978), pp. 237–61; M.J. Sodaro, 'Soviet Studies of the Western Alliance', in H.J. Ellison (ed.), *Soviet Policy towards Western Europe* (Seattle, WA, University of Washington, 1983).

Chapter 2

1 M.K. Bunkina, *USA versus Western Europe: New Trends* (Moscow, Progress, 1979), pp. 11, 18; Binns, 'From USE to EEC', p. 251. In contemporary debates, Lenin tended to stress conflictual aspects. V.I. Lenin, 'Imperialism, the Highest Stage of Capitalism', *Selected Works* (London, Lawrence and Wishart, 1969), pp. 237, 256–7.

2 Gorbachev, *Politicheskii doklad*, pp. 17–18, 20; the frustration which Soviet ambiguities can generate in Western researchers is reflected in Sodaro, 'Soviet Studies of the Western Alliance', e.g. on p. 8.

3 Yu.V. Shishkov, D.E. Mel'nikov, V.G. Baranovsky, 'Istoricheskie predposylki i dvizhushchie sily integratsionnykh protsessov v Zapadnoi Evrope', in N.S. Kishilov (ed.), *Zapadnoevropeiskaya integratsiya: politicheskie aspekty* (Moscow, Nauka, 1985), pp. 17–22; Yu.V. Shishkov, *Formirovanie integratsionnogo kompleksa v Zapadnoi Evrope: tendentsii i protivorechii* (Moscow, Nauka, 1979), pp. 13–14; V.G. Baranovsky, *Politicheskaya integratsiya v Zapadnoi Evrope* (Moscow, Nauka, 1983), pp. 94–5; A. Shapiro, *MEMO*, 1985, no. 3, pp. 91–102; M. Bunkina, V. Petrov, *MEMO*, 1986, no. 9, pp. 49–57; Yu. Shishkov, *MEMO*, 1987, no. 11, pp. 91–101; for a more conservative view, see E. Pletnev, *MEMO*, 1985, no. 7, pp. 106–13.

4 B. Parrott, *Politics and Technology in the Soviet Union* (London, MIT Press, 1985), p. 139; Shishkov, *MEMO*, 1987, no. 11, pp. 100–101; Bunkina, Petrov, *MEMO*, 1986, no. 9, pp. 54, 56. Some continue to dissent: see Yu. Shiryaev, *Social Sciences*, 1986, no. 1, pp. 86–7.

5 F. Barghoorn, 'The Varga Discussion and its Significance', *American Slavic and East European Review*, vol. 6 (1948), pp. 214–36; Parrott, *Politics and Technology in the Soviet Union*, pp. 82–8.

6 Parrott, *Politics and Technology in the Soviet Union*, pp. 149, 233, 249, 267–8; Binns, 'From USE to EEC', pp. 257–9.

7 A. Bykova, N. Shmelev, *MEMO*, 1986, no. 9, pp. 67–9; V. V. Razmerov, Yu.E. Fedorov, *MEMO*, 1988, no. 1, pp. 5–7.

8 Shapiro, *MEMO*, 1985, no. 3, pp. 30–32; Shapiro refers in particular to R. Keohane, J. Nye, *Power and Interdependence: World Politics in Transition* (Boston, MA, Little, Brown, 1977). Cf. M.A. Maksimova, *MEMO*, 1978, no. 4, p. 17.

9 N. Shmelev, *International Affairs* (Moscow), 1985, no. 9; I. Osadchaya, *MEMO*, 1987, no. 10, p. 27; V. Zuev at round-table in *MEMO*, 1987, no. 3, p. 94; A. Bovin, V. Lukin, *MEMO*, 1987, no. 12, pp. 57–8; Bunkina, Petrov, *MEMO*, 1986, no. 9, p. 53.

10 See, for instance, Ya. Pevszner's criticism of Lester Thurow. *MEMO*, 1986, no. 10, p. 103; Lester Thurow, 'A Time to Dismantle the World Economy', *The Economist*, 9 November 1985; reprinted in translation in *MEMO*, 1986, no. 10.

11 A. Shapiro, *SShA*, 1985, no. 3, p. 32.

12 Maksimova, *MEMO*, 1978, no. 4, p. 18. Also Yu. Borko, *MEMO*, 1988, no. 2, p. 48.

13 Shishkov, *Formirovanie integratsionnogo kompleksa*, p. 21.

14 T. Kosyreva, *MEMO*, 1988, no. 1, pp. 143–5.

15 V.P. Lukin, '*Tsentry sily'. Kontseptsii i real'nost'* (Moscow, Mezhdunarodnye otnosheniya, 1983), pp. 17, 95. Lukin's writing does not carry the political charge of the work of someone like Yakovlev. Another example of academic 'regionalism' is A. Borodaevsky's 'Internationalisation and Economic Integration in the Capitalist World', *Social Sciences*, 1985, no. 2, pp. 81–93. On 'power-centres' see M. Maksimova, *MEMO*, 1978, no. 4, p. 18; Binns, 'From USE to EEC', p. 253; Bunkina, *USA versus Western Europe*, pp. 32–3. See also Mel'nikov, *MEMO*, 1978, no. 5, p. 19; V. B. Knyazhinsky (ed.), *Zapadnoevropeiskaya integratsiya: proekty i real'nost'* (Moscow, Mezhdunarodnye otnosheniya, 1986), pp. 5, 165.

16 A. Yakovlev, *Kommunist*, 1986, no. 17, p. 9; A. Yakovlev, *Pravda*, 23 March 1984.

17 *Kommunist*, 1986, no. 17, p. 13. See also the author's criticism of American militarism, mass anti-Soviet hysteria, and 'bourgeois state totalitarianism' in *SShA*, 1985, no. 3, pp. 3–4, 15; J. Hough, 'Soviet Perspectives on European Security', pp. 39–41; Hough, *The Struggle for the Third World*, pp. 223–4.

18 *Kommunist*, 1986, no. 17, pp. 15–16.

19 Razmerov, Fedorov, *MEMO*, 1988, no. 1, p. 6. Much of this article is commentary on Gorbachev's speech on the 70th anniversary of the

October Revolution, which is similarly 'internationalist' in tone. *Izvestiya*, 3 November 1987.

20 V.I. Lenin, 'The Socialist Revolution and the Right of Nations to Self-Determination', *Selected Works*, p. 157. In this Soviet internationalism resembles Western varieties. See F. Halliday, 'Three concepts of internationalism', *International Affairs* (London), vol. 64, no. 2 (1988), pp. 187–98. The internationalism discussed here is, it should be said, a different thing from the 'revolutionary internationalism' discussed in Halliday's article.

21 Bovin, Lukin, *MEMO*, 1987, no. 12, pp. 56, 58. See, too, the references to the muting of inter-imperialist conflict in Gorbachev's speech on the 70th anniversary of the October Revolution, *Izvestiya*, 3 November 1987. Adomeit saw evidence of the emergence of similar views towards the end of the 1970s. 'Soviet Perceptions of Western European Integration', pp. 8, 11–13.

Chapter 3

1 Yu. Borko, *MEMO*, 1988, no. 2, p. 35.

2 Binns, 'From USE to EEC', p. 238; V.I. Lenin, 'On the Slogan for a United States of Europe', *Selected Works*, pp. 154–5.

3 'O sozdanii "obshchego rynka" i Evratoma (Tezisy)', *MEMO*, 1957, no. 1, pp. 83–96. Binns demonstrates that this was a compromise document, parts of which were much less dismissive of the EEC. Binns, 'From USE to EEC', pp. 246–50.

4 Traditional 'class analysis' is still to be encountered even in an academic context, but usually in historical writing or when topics such as the enlargement of the Community are under discussion. Shishkov, Mel'nikov, Baranovsky, 'Istoricheskie predposylki', pp. 30–42; Knyazhinsky (ed.), *Zapadnoevropeiskaya integratsiya*, pp. 5, 124, 132, 152–4, 195; Shishkov, *Formirovanie integratsionnogo kompleksa*, p. 216; V. Kniazhinsky [sic], *West European Integration: Its Policies and International Relations* (Moscow, Progress, 1984), pp. 110–11; Baranovsky, *Politicheskaya integratsiya v Zapadnoi Evrope*, p. 13; V. Lavrenov, *MEMO*, 1978, no. 6, p. 55–7; Adomeit, 'Soviet Perceptions', 1979, no. 1, p. 15; Knyazhinsky (ed.), *Zapadnoevropeiskaya integratsiya*, pp. 152–4. West European Communist Party opposition to supranational developments is also echoed. Kniazhinsky, *West European Integration*, pp. 247, 249; D.D. Maklein *et al.*, 'Problemy politicheskoi integratsii i pozitsiya zapadnoevropeiskikh gosudarstv', in Kishilov (ed.), *Zapadnoevropeiskaya integratsiya*, p. 51; Baranovsky, *Politicheskaya integratsiya v Zapadnoi Evrope*, p. 203.

5 Binns, 'From USE to EEC', pp. 249–60.

6 Baranovsky, *Politicheskaya integratsiya v Zapadnoi Evrope*, p. 54;

M.M. Maksimova, *Osnovnye problemy imperialisticheskoi integratsii.
Ekonomicheskii aspekt* (Moscow, Nauka, 1971), p. 333.

7 Baranovsky, *Politicheskaya integratsiya v Zapadnoi Evrope*, pp. 196–7,
215, 226–30. See also Mel'nikov, *MEMO*, 1978, no. 5, p. 23; Adomeit,
'Soviet Perceptions', p. 10. Shishkov, Mel'nikov and Baranovsky
divide the motive forces of West European integration into economic,
socio-political and international-political. 'Istoricheskie predposylki',
pp. 25–9, 44–6. See too Knyazhinsky (ed.), *Zapadnoevropeiskaya
integratsiya*, pp. 152–4.

8 Borko, *MEMO*, 1988, no. 2, p. 37. On the same page Borko states
that social-democratic parties 'dominate in the workers' movement of
almost all West European countries'.

9 Borko, *MEMO*, 1988, no. 2, pp. 37–41.

10 Borko, *MEMO*, 1988, no. 2, pp. 44–6. The idea of the possibility of
democratizing the EC from within has been present in Soviet commentary for many years, as it has in the programmes of certain
Western communist parties, but in the past it has not been so strongly
expressed. Cf. Binns, 'From USE to EEC', p. 256; Shishkov, *Formirovanie integratsionnogo kompleksa*, pp. 339–40; Kniazhinsky, *West
European Integration*, pp. 268–9.

11 Adomeit, 'Soviet Perceptions', p. 21.

12 Maksimova, *Osnovnye problemy imperialisticheskoi integratsii*, p. 208;
Baranovsky, *Politicheskaya integratsiya v Zapadnoi Evrope*, pp. 46,
175–6. See also V.G. Baranovsky, 'Politicheskii mekhanizm
evropeiskogo soobshchestva', in Kishilov (ed.), *Zapadnoevropeiskaya
integratsiya*, p. 119; Knyazhinsky (ed.), *Zapadnoevropeiskaya integratsiya*, pp. 161–7; Kniazhinsky, *West European Integration*, pp. 202,
211.

13 Baranovsky, *Politicheskaya integratsiya v Zapadnoi Evrope*, p. 174;
Yu.P. Davydov, 'Dva "tsentra sily" v mirovoi politike i problema
razryadki', in Yu.P. Davydov (ed.), *SShA-Zapadnaya Evropa i problema razryadki* (Moscow, Nauka, 1986), p. 9.

14 Kniazhinsky, *West European Integration*, p. 208; Borko, *MEMO*,
1988, no. 2, p. 47. See also Baranovsky, 'Politicheskii mekhanizm', p.
122; Baranovsky, *Politicheskaya integratsiya v Zapadnoi Evrope*, p. 28;
Mel'nikov, *MEMO*, 1978, no. 5, pp. 23–8.

15 Baranovsky, *Politicheskaya integratsiya v Zapadnoi Evrope*, pp. 28,
175; see also Rubinsky, *MEMO*, 1987, no. 12, p. 86; Yu. Davydov,
'Dva "tsentra sily"', p. 9; Yu. Chistov at the round-table in *MEMO*,
1987, no. 5, p. 103.

16 Rubinsky, *MEMO*, 1987, no. 12, pp. 86, 90.

17 S. Karaganov, *Moscow News*, 1988, no. 34, p. 3. See also Mel'nikov,

MEMO, 1978, no. 5, p. 23; Baranovsky, 'Politicheskii mekhanizm', pp. 131–3; Rubinsky, *MEMO*, 1987, no. 12, p. 90.

18 S. Vybornov, A. Gusenkov, V. Leontiev, *International Affairs* (Moscow), 1988, no. 3, p. 36.

19 Kniazhinsky, *West European Integration*, pp. 213–29, 273–6, 302; Maklein *et al.*, 'Problemy politicheskoi integratsii', pp. 54–78; Baranovsky, *Politicheskaya integratsiya v Zapadnoi Evrope*, pp. 20–23, 173, 197, 215; Knyazhinsky (ed.), *Zapadnoevropeiskaya integratsiya*, pp. 148, 173.

20 Mel'nikov, *MEMO*, 1978, no. 5, pp. 78–9; Davydov, 'Dva "tsentra sily"', p. 9. See also Maksimova, *MEMO*, 1978, no. 4, p. 21; V. Zuev at the round-table in *MEMO*, 1987, no. 5, p. 94; Knyazhinsky (ed.), *Zapadnoevropeiskaya integratsiya*, p. 132; Kniazhinsky, *West European Integration*, pp. 287, 290–1, 233–6.

21 Baranovsky, *Politicheskaya integratsiya v Zapadnoi Evrope*, p. 256; Knyazhinsky (ed.), *Zapadnoevropeiskaya integratsiya*, p. 134.

22 E. Pozdnyakov, *MEMO*, 1987, no. 10, pp. 36–7 (emphasis in original). See also V.G. Baranovsky, *Evropeiskoe soobshchestvo v sisteme mezhdunarodnykh otnoshenii* (Moscow, Nauka, 1986).

23 Rubinsky, *MEMO*, 1987, no. 12, p. 90; Borko, *MEMO*, 1988, no. 2, p. 42; Knyazhinsky (ed.), *Zapadnoevropeiskaya integratsiya*, pp. 96–8; Zuev, Korovkin, Tsimailo and Chistov in the round-table discussion in *MEMO*, 1987, no. 5, pp. 94–7.

24 Nerushenko in the round-table discussion in *MEMO*, 1987, no. 5, pp. 95–6.

25 A. Kudryavtsev, *MEMO*, 1986, no. 10, p. 31. Shishkov, *Formirovanie integratsionnogo kompleksa*, p. 39; Kniazhinsky, *West European Integration*, pp. 147, 154–5.

26 Contributions by V. Zuev, N. Shulyukin, N. Shelyubskaya, V. Chistov, *MEMO*, 1987, no. 5, pp. 95–7, 103; A. Bykova and N. Shmelev explicitly recommend West European programmes as a model of efficiency. *MEMO*, 1986, no. 9, pp. 64, 68–9.

27 See Chapter 2.

28 V. Pripisnov, *MEMO*, 1987, no. 5, p. 97; see also contributions by Ya. Zaslavsky, N. Krichigina, M. Bunkina, on pp. 97–8; I. Ponomareva, N. Smirnova, *MEMO*, 1986, no. 8, p. 136. The comment about the erosion of the nucleus of monopoly capital was made by Kapustin in the discussion in *MEMO*, 1987, no. 5, p. 98.

29 Yu. Shishkov, 'Integratsiya khozyaistvennoi politiki', in Kishilov (ed.), *Zapadnoevropeiskaya integratsiya*, esp. pp. 173–4; Shishkov, *International Affairs* (Moscow), 1985, no. 10, pp. 64–73; Shishkov, *MEMO*, 1986, no. 6, pp. 40–53.

30 V. Shenaev, *MEMO*, 1988, no. 2, p. 132.

31 A. Khlystov, *MEMO*, 1988, no. 2, p. 132. See also Razmerov, Fedorov, *MEMO*, 1988, no. 1, p. 7; Ponomareva, Smirnova, *MEMO*, 1986, no. 8, p. 32.

32 V. Tsirenshchikov, N. Krichigina, A. Fesenko, V. Shul'tseva, A. Grigor'ev, L. Fedorova, in *MEMO*, 1988, no. 2, p. 133.

33 A. Kudryavtsev, *MEMO*, 1986, no. 10, pp. 26–41; Yu. Yudanov, *MEMO*, 1986, no. 9, pp. 93–100; V. Presnyakov, T. Yudina, L. Glukharev, V. Slavinsky in the round-table discussion, *MEMO*, 1988, no. 2, pp. 132–4.

34 V. Pan'kov, *MEMO*, 1987, no. 10, p. 123.

35 V. Prokudin, Yu. Andreev, S. Fedyukin, *MEMO*, 1988, no. 2, p. 135.

36 *International Affairs* (Moscow), 1985, no. 10, p. 69.

37 Bunkina, *USA versus Western Europe*, p. 6; Shishkov, *Formirovanie integratsionnogo kompleksa*, p. 332. See also Adomeit, 'Soviet Perceptions', p. 10; Mel'nikov, *MEMO*, 1978, no. 5, pp. 19–21, 29.

38 Bunkina, *USA versus Western Europe*, pp. 6–7 (English in original).

39 Adomeit, 'Soviet Perceptions', pp. 10–11; Mel'nikov, *MEMO*, 1978, no. 5, p. 22; Yu.P. Davydov, *SShA*, 1975, no. 6, p. 36; Maksimova, *MEMO*, 1978, no. 4, pp. 14–18; Bunkina, *USA versus Western Europe*, p. 7.

40 Bykova, Shmelev, *MEMO*, 1986, no. 9, p. 62. The authors emphasize the special contribution made by the USA's large number of small high-technology firms.

41 Razmerov, Fedorov, *MEMO*, 1988, no. 1, p. 7; V. Pripisnov and V. Shul'tseva's contributions to the discussion in *MEMO*, 1987, no. 5, pp. 97, 99; N. Shelyubskaya and B. Komzin's in *MEMO*, 1988, no. 2, p. 133. Bunkina, however, denied that the lag was worsening. *MEMO*, 1987, no. 5, p. 97.

42 Ponomareva, Smirnova, *MEMO*, 1986, no. 8, pp. 91–6; Shishkov, *MEMO*, 1986, no. 6, p. 46; Yakovlev, *Kommunist*, 1986, no. 17, p. 86.

43 Kudryavtsev, *MEMO*, 1986, no. 10, pp. 26–40; contributions by N. Krichigina and V. Kapustin to the round-table discussion in *MEMO*, 1987, no. 5, p. 98; Rubinsky, *MEMO*, 1987, no. 12, p. 85; Davydov, 'Dva "tsentra sily"', pp. 18–19.

44 Yu. Yudanov, *MEMO*, 1986, no. 9, pp. 93–100; Yu. Stolyarov, E. Khesin, *MEMO*, 1987, no. 5, p. 27; Bykova, Shmelev, *MEMO*, 1986, no. 9, pp. 63–4; V. Presnyakov's contribution to the round-table discussion in *MEMO*, 1987, no. 5, p. 96.

45 Vtorov, Karelov, *International Affairs* (Moscow), 1986, no. 6, p. 98 (English in original). Hough identifies Vtorov as Anatoly Kovalev in 'Soviet Perspectives on European Security', p. 25. His role in Soviet diplomacy in the 1970s is described in A.N. Shevchenko, *Breaking with Moscow* (New York, NY, Knopf, 1985), pp. 265–7.

46 *Kommunist*, 1986, no. 17, p. 8; *Pravda*, 23 March 1984. Cf. Kniazhinsky, *West European Integration*, pp. 163–4.

47 V. Zagladin on Soviet Television, 'Studio Nine', 6 February 1988, *Summary of World Broadcasts*, SU/0069, p. A1/3 (8 February 1988).

48 Pan'kov, *MEMO*, 1987, no. 10, p. 124. See V.N. Rynza on the Brandt Commission Report, 'Vneevropeiskie faktory: vliyanie na razryadku', Yu.P. Davydov (ed.), *SShA – Zapadnaya Evropa i problema razryadki* (Moscow, Nauka, 1986), pp. 108–9; Borko, *MEMO*, 1988, no. 2, p. 49; Borko on social policies in Western Europe, *MEMO*, 1988, no. 5, pp. 134–9; Yu. Krasin on the possibilities for political collaboration on the left, in *MEMO*, 1988, no. 4, pp. 23–33; Yu. Borko, B. Orlov, *MEMO*, 1988, no. 9, pp. 46–58.

Chapter 4

1 Adomeit, 'Soviet Perceptions', pp. 9–13; Binns, 'From USE to EEC'; Shishkov, *Formirovanie integratsionnogo kompleksa*, p. 24; Baranovsky, *Politicheskaya integratsiya v Zapadnoi Evrope*, pp. 211–13.

2 Lukin, '*Tsentry sily*', pp. 26–7; S. Karaganov, 'Voennaya strategiya SShA i NATO i otnosheniya mezhdu Vostokom i Zapadom', in Yu. Davydov (ed.), *SShA – Zapadnaya Evropa i problema razryadki*, p. 167.

3 A. Kunitsyn, 'Torgovlya Vostok-Zapad: politika i kommertsiya', in Yu. Davydov (ed.), *SShA – Zapadnaya Evropa i problema razryadki*, pp. 125–9; Kniazhinsky, *West European Integration*, p. 332.

4 In 'Dva "tsentra sily"', p. 13; see, too, Lukin, '*Tsentry sily*', pp. 48–9. The decline of military intervention as a usable option in the Third World during the 1970s was held to have allowed more scope for West European influence. V. Rynza, 'Vneevropeiskie faktory: vliyanie na razryadku', in Yu. Davydov (ed.), *SShA – Zapadnaya Evropa i problema razryadki*, pp. 109–11.

5 P. T. Podlesny, 'Faktor Sovetskogo Soyuza v amerikano-zapad-noevropeiskikh otnosheniyakh', in Yu. Davydov (ed.), *SShA – Zapadnaya Evropa i problema razryadki*, p. 47.

6 Yu. Davydov, 'Obshchee i spetsificheskoe v podkhodakh SShA i Zapadnoi Evropy', in Yu. Davydov (ed.), *SShA – Zapadnaya Evropa i problema razryadki*.

7 Lukin, '*Tsentry sily*', p. 65; A.I. Utkin, *Doktriny atlantizma i evropeiskaya integratsiya* (Moscow, Nauka, 1979), p. 73; Kniazhinsky, *West European Integration*, pp. 304–5; 298–9, 348; Knyazhinsky (ed.), *Zapadnoevropeiskaya integratsiya*, p. 126. Various writers have their own conceptions of 'Europeanism'. Knyazhinsky's is peculiarly (and wishfully) pan-European in colouring.

8 Borko, *MEMO*, 1988, no. 2, p. 49.

9 See Mel'nikov, *MEMO* 1978, no. 5, p. 26; Adomeit, 'Soviet Perceptions', pp. 10–11; Sodaro, 'Soviet Studies of the Western Alliance', p. 247. The 24th CPSU Congress Report in 1971 already spoke of 'ever more acute struggle' between the three main centres of imperialism.

10 V. Shein, 'Razryadka i Severoatlanticheskii blok', in Yu. Davydov (ed.), *SShA – Zapadnaya Evropa i problema razryadki*, p. 147.

11 Yakovlev, *Pravda*, 23 March 1984; Yakovlev, *Kommunist*, 1986, no. 17, pp. 3–17; Shishkov, *International Affairs* (Moscow), 1986, no. 5, pp. 28–36; Podlesny, 'Faktor Sovetskogo Soyuza', p. 48, citing F. Halliday, *The Making of the Second Cold War* (London, Verso, 1983), p. 179. There is no debate, as in the West, over whether the Cold War was aimed mainly at allies *or* at ostensible enemies. See the work by Halliday already cited, and M. Cox, 'The Cold War as a System', *Critique*, no. 17 (1986), pp. 17–82.

12 Yu. Davydov, *SShA*, 1985, no. 8, pp. 51–3; Vorontsov, *SShA*, 1984, no. 4, pp. 3–13; Ponomareva, Smirnova, *MEMO*, 1986, no. 8, pp. 131–6; Yakovlev, *Pravda*, 23 March 1984; Shishkov, *International Affairs* (Moscow), 1986, no. 5, pp. 28–36; Knyazhinsky (ed.), *Zapadnoevropeiskaya integratsiya*, p. 117; Kniazhinsky, *West European Integration*, pp. 322–6; Kirichenko, *International Affairs* (Moscow), 1985, no. 6, pp. 82–6, 106; Zimenkov, Parkansky, *SShA*, 1985, no. 10, pp. 21–5; Yu. Davydov, 'Dva "tsentra sily"', pp. 18–21.

13 Shein, 'Razryadka i Severoatlanticheskii blok', pp. 162–5. See also Yakovlev, *SShA*, 1985, no. 7, pp. 10–11; Kniazhinsky, *West European Integration*, pp. 283–6, 330–5; A. Pisarev, 'Obshcheevropeiskii protsess: konfrontatsiya ili sotrudnichestvo?', in Yu. Davydov (ed.), *SShA – Zapadnaya Evropa i problema razryadki*, p. 67; Baranovsky, *Politicheskaya integratsiya v Zapadnoi Evrope*, pp. 253–5.

14 Lukin, *'Tsentry Sily'*, pp. 79, 82, 87, 89; R. F. Laird, 'Soviet Perspectives on French Security Policy', *Survival*, vol. 27, no. 2 (1985), p. 70. Knyazhinsky likewise wrote of the emergence of a tendency to create a relatively autonomous centre of power in the military sphere, although he acknowledged that in the immediate future this would essentially come down to a shift in the balance inside NATO. *West European Integration*, pp. 346–8; 379–83. Sodaro notes that in 1966 it was being predicted in the USSR that de Gaulle's move could snowball into the establishing of a separate European defence identity. Sodaro, 'Soviet Studies of the Western Alliance', p. 246. More sceptical views from the 1970s are cited in Adomeit, 'Soviet Perceptions', p. 18; Sodaro, 'Soviet Studies of the Western Alliance', pp. 254–5.

15 Kniazhinsky, *West European Integration*, pp. 379–80; Lukin, *'Tsentry sily'*, pp. 84–5; Knyazhinsky (ed.), *Zapadnoevropeiskaya integratsiya*, pp. 135–9; Parkhalina, *MEMO*, 1986, no. 7, p. 106.

16 Kolosov, *Voenno-politicheskii kurs Anglii*, p. 239.
17 Laird, 'Soviet Perspectives on French Security Policy', p. 71;
Kniazhinsky, *West European Integration*, p. 348; see, too,
Knyazhinsky (ed.), *Zapadnoevropeiskaya integratsiya*, p. 144. Pierre
Hassner raises the possibility that Moscow, having accepted West
European economic integration, is now 'at the borderline of the political and the military', but rejects it. Hassner, 'Europe between the
USA and the USSR', p. 29. See also Laird, 'Soviet Perspectives on
French Security Policy', pp. 70–2.
18 Kniazhinsky, *West European Integration*, p. 389; Yakovlev, *SShA*,
1985, no. 7, p. 13 (cf. Podlesny, 'Faktor Sovetskogo Soyuza', p. 51);
Yakovlev, *Kommunist*, 1986, no. 17, pp. 16–17.
19 Yakovlev, *Kommunist*, 1986, no. 17, p. 8.
20 Yu. Davydov, *SShA*, 1987, no. 5, p. 8.
21 Davydov, 'Dva "tsentra sily"', p. 12 (also 'Obshchee i spetsificheskoe', pp. 23–4); Yu. Davydov, *SShA*, 1987, no. 5, p. 8; also
Pisarev, 'Obshcheevropeiskii protsess', p. 67; Presnyakov,
Iordanskaya, *MEMO*, 1987, no. 11, p. 89; V. Mil'shtein, *MEMO*,
1988, no. 1, pp. 148–9; Parkhalina, *MEMO*, 1986, no. 7, p. 110. See
also V. Razmerov, Yu. Fedorov, *MEMO*, 1988, no. 1, pp. 8–10.
22 V. Razmerov, Yu. Fedorov, *MEMO*, 1988, no. 1, pp. 8–11.
23 Respectively E. Pozdnyakov, *MEMO*, 1987, no. 11, p. 38; Parkhalina,
MEMO, 1986, no. 7, p. 110; Davydov, 'Dva "tsentra sily"', pp. 6, 18.
24 For earlier statements, see Mel'nikov, *MEMO*, 1978, no. 5, p. 25;
Adomeit, 'Soviet Perspectives', p. 20.
25 Kolosov, *Voenno-politicheskii kurs Anglii*, pp. 76–80, 169, 199–200,
238.
26 G. Kolosov, 'Voenno-politicheskie aspekty zapadnoevropeiskogo
integratsionnogo protsessa', in Kishilov (ed.), *Zapadnoevropeiskaya
integratsiya*, p. 241. See, too, pp. 245–55; Davydov, 'Dva "tsentra
sily"', pp. 12–13; A. Yakovlev, *Pravda*, 23 March 1984; Mel'nikov
MEMO, 1978, no. 3, p. 26; for a recent restatement, see Razmerov,
Fedorov, *MEMO*, 1988, no. 1, p. 8.
27 V. Kudryavtsev, *MEMO*, 1986, no. 10, pp. 26–40; Yu. Yudanov,
MEMO, 1986, no. 9, pp. 93–100; Razmerov, Fedorov, *MEMO*, 1988,
no. 1, pp. 14–16; V. Stupishin, *International Affairs* (Moscow), 1988,
no. 5, p. 72; round-table discussion in *MEMO*, 1988, no. 2, pp. 129ff,
especially contributions by R. Shchenin, A. Arbatov, D. Melamid *et
al.*, A. Shein, M. Bogdanov, A. Chervyakov.
28 A. Beletsky, *International Affairs* (Moscow), 1986, no. 6, p. 55; round-
table discussion in *MEMO*, 1988, no. 2, p. 132: contributions by A.
Kalyadin and G. Kolosov, Yu. Kostko.
29 Knyazhinsky (ed.), *Zapadnoevropeiskaya integratsiya*, p. 143.

30 *Pravda*, 5 May 1984, cited in Hough, 'Soviet Perspectives on European Security', pp. 27–8. See also Knyazhinsky (ed.), *Zapadnoevropeiskaya integratsiya*, pp. 141–7; Vidyasova, *International Affairs* (Moscow), 1985, no. 6, pp. 106–11. See Parkhalina's reference (*MEMO*, 1986, no. 7, p. 107) to Henry Kissinger's proposals for adjustments in alliance roles in *Time*, 5 March 1984, and Stanley Hoffman's in *Foreign Affairs*, Winter 1981/2, pp. 327–46.

31 Yakovlev, *SShA*, 1985, no. 7, pp. 3–10; Valentin Falin, Moscow's ex-ambassador to Bonn, by then head of APN, described American policy as 'the godfather of neo-revanchism' in Germany. *MEMO*, 1987, no. 12, p. 77. See also Yakovlev in *Pravda*, 23 March 1984.

32 Kolosov, 'Voenno-politicheskie aspekty', p. 241.

33 See Yu. Davydov, 'Dva "tsentra sily"', p. 6: 'Washington's striving for hegemony hampered (without stoppping) the process' of growing independence; also p. 18.

34 Razmerov, Fedorov, *MEMO*, 1988, no. 1, pp. 10–12. Cf. Yu. Davydov, 'Dva "tsentra sily"', pp. 3, 15; Yu. Davydov, 'Obshchee i spetsificheskoe', p. 39; Podlesny, 'Faktor Sovetskogo Soyuza', p. 44.

35 V. Mikheev, 'Levye sily i otnosheniya Vostok-Zapad' in Yu. Davydov (ed.), *SShA – Zapadnaya Evropa i problema razryadki*, p. 79; Borko, *MEMO*, 1988, no. 2, p. 49; Knyazhinsky (ed.), *Zapadnoevropeiskaya integratsiya*, pp. 174–5; Pan'kov, *MEMO*, 1987, no. 10, pp. 121–5; A. Grigoryants, *International Affairs* (Moscow), 1986, no. 4, pp. 81–9.

36 Shein, 'Razryadka i Severoatlanticheskii blok', pp. 147–64; H. Kissinger, *The White House Years* (London, Weidenfeld and Nicolson, 1979), p. 224; see articles by Yakovlev already referred to, esp. *SShA*, 1985, no. 7, pp. 11–13.

37 Davydov, *SShA*, 1987, no. 5, pp. 3–14.

38 Razmerov, Fedorov, *MEMO*, 1988, no. 1, p. 12.

39 Podlesny, 'Faktor Sovetskogo Soyuza', p. 49; Karaganov, 'Voennaya strategiya SShA i NATO', p. 167–93; Razmerov, Fedorov, *MEMO*, 1988, no. 1, pp. 8–19; Kolosov, *Voenno-politicheskii kurs Anglii*, pp. 20–7; Davydov, *SShA*, 1987, no. 5, pp. 8–10. Avakov *et al.* provide a comprehensive summary of the strategic debates inside NATO in 1987–8 in *MEMO*, 1988, no. 7, pp. 70–6. The new willingness to acknowledge widespread apprehension of a Soviet threat means that these accounts are coming more and more to resemble Western ones.

40 Kolosov, *Voenno-politicheskii kurs Anglii*, pp. 39–48; V.G. Trukhanovsky, N.K. Kapitonova, *Sovetsko-angliiskie otnosheniya 1945–1978* (Moscow, Mezhdunarodnye otnosheniya, 1979); S. Volodin, *International Affairs* (Moscow), 1982, no. 3, pp. 31–40; V. Amirov, B. Bolotin, O. Ivanova, Yu. Krashennikov, *MEMO*, 1986, no. 10, p. 73.

41 Vtorov, *International Affairs* (Moscow), 1985, no. 12, pp. 3–5. Vtorov is the pseudonym of Kovalev (see note 45, Chapter 3). See also Tyulin, *International Affairs* (Moscow), 1984, no. 4, p. 137; Mikheev, 'Levye sily', p. 79; Kniazhinsky, *West European Integration*, pp. 299–301.

42 Davydov, 'Obshchee i spetsificheskoe', p. 25; R. Laird, 'Soviet Perspectives on French Security Policy', *Survival*, vol. 27, no. 2 (1985), pp. 67–72.

43 N. Afanasevsky, E. Tarasinkevich, A. Shvedov, *International Affairs* (Moscow), 1988, no. 5, pp. 22–33; also S. Vybornov, A. Gusenkov, V. Leontiev, *International Affairs* (Moscow), 1988, no. 3, pp. 35–6 (in English).

44 See especially the contributions by G. Kolosov, A. Chervyakov, *MEMO*, 1987, no. 5, pp. 100–101.

45 Contributions by R. Shchenin, E. Talyzina, *MEMO*, 1987, no. 5, pp. 100–101.

46 Vladimir Stupishin, Principal Advisor of the Evaluations and Planning Directorate, *International Affairs* (Moscow), 1988, no. 5, p. 72 (in English).

47 S. Karaganov, *SShA*, 1987, no. 10, pp. 25–34.

48 Shevardnadze in July 1988: 'The 19th All-Union CPSU Conference: Foreign Policy and Diplomacy', *International Affairs* (Moscow), 1988, no. 10, p. 10 (see also pp. 36–7); V. Zagladin on Soviet Television, 'Studio Nine', 6 February 1988, *Summary of World Broadcasts*, SU/0069, p. A1/3 (8 February 1988). See too the next chapter.

49 Vybornov, Gusenkov, Leontiev, *International Affairs* (Moscow), 1988, no. 3, pp. 36–7.

50 Vybornov, Gusenkov, Leontiev, *International Affairs* (Moscow), 1988, no. 3, p. 37.

51 Stupishin, *International Affairs* (Moscow), 1988, no. 5, p. 73 (in English).

52 Karaganov, *SShA*, 1987, no. 10, pp. 25–34. Others proposed quite explicitly that further concessions should be made in order to calm West European apprehensions. M. Maksimova, *MEMO*, 1988, no. 10, p. 63.

53 Kirillov, *International Affairs* (Moscow), 1986, no. 4, p. 59; Amirov *et al.*, *MEMO*, 1986, no. 10, p. 73; Wettig, 'The Soviet View', pp. 45–6. German 'Atlanticism' has been a perennial topic for complaint by Soviet writers. Sodaro, 'Soviet Studies of the Western Alliance', p. 257.

54 Yu. Yudanov, *MEMO*, 1988, no. 9, p. 91.

55 Zagladin on Soviet Television, 'Studio Nine', 6 February 1988, *Summary of World Broadcasts*, SU/0069, pp. A1/4, 5 (8 February 1988);

E. Grigor'ev (deputy editor of *Pravda*) on Soviet Television, 'Rezonans', 7 April 1988, *Summary of World Broadcasts*, SU/0127, p. A1/5 (16 April 1988).

56 Zagladin, *Summary of World Broadcasts*, SU/0069, pp. A1/4, 5; Yudanov, *MEMO*, 1988, no. 9, pp. 91–2.

57 M. Maksimova, *MEMO*, 1988, no. 10, p. 64.

58 *Pravda*, 24 April 1988.

59 Maksimova, *MEMO*, 1988, no. 10, pp. 63–5. Maksimova also proposes large-scale academic collaboration between the USSR and West Germany.

60 Mikhailov, *Pravda*, 24 April 1988; Yudanov, *MEMO*, 1988, no. 9, p. 92. Similar warnings were issued by V. Varnavsky, *MEMO*, 1987, no. 11, pp. 133–6; V. Falin, *MEMO*, 1987, no. 12, pp. 73–84.

61 Zagladin, *Summary of World Broadcasts*, SU/0069, p. A1/5 (8 February 1988).

Chapter 5

1 D. Simes, 'The Politics of Defense in the Soviet Union: Brezhnev's Era', in J. Valenta, W.C. Potter (eds.), *Soviet Decisionmaking for National Security* (London, Allen and Unwin, 1984), p. 79; F. Griffiths, 'Ideological Development and Foreign Policy', in S. Bialer (ed.), *The Domestic Context of Soviet Foreign Policy* (London, Croom Helm, 1981), p. 20; J. Hough, 'The Evolution of the Soviet World View', *World Politics*, vol. 32 (1980), pp. 509–30.

2 Jack Snyder describes this as a period of 'offensive detente'. 'The Gorbachev Revolution: A Waning of Soviet Expansionism?', *International Security*, vol. 12, no. 3 (1987–8), pp. 93–131; H. Gelman, *The Brezhnev Politburo and the Decline of Detente* (London, Cornell University, 1984), p. 155; Hough, *Struggle for the Third World*; 'Perestroika, the 19th Party Conference and Foreign Policy', *International Affairs* (Moscow), 1988, no. 7, pp. 13–15.

3 Reassessments were already going on in the first half of the 1980s, especially during Andropov's period in office. F. Fukuyama, 'Gorbachev and the Third World', *Foreign Affairs*, vol. 64, no. 4 (1986), pp. 715–22.

4 C. Glickham, 'New Directions for Soviet Foreign Policy', *Radio Liberty Research Supplement*, 2/86 (6 April 1986); Snyder, 'The Gorbachev Revolution', pp. 108–10; A. Rahr, 'Gorbachev's Personal Staff', *Radio Liberty Research Report*, 2 June 1986; S. Akhromeev, *Sovetskaya Rossiya*, 21 February 1987; S. Akhromeev, *Krasnaya zvezda*, 9 May 1987; D. Yazov, *Pravda*, 27 July 1987.

5 Gorbachev, 'Oktyabr' i perestroika', *Izvestiya*, 3 November 1987; E. Primakov, 'Novaya filosofiya vneshnei politiki', *Pravda*, 10 July

1987; S. Shenfield, *The Nuclear Predicament: Explorations in Soviet Ideology* (London, Routledge for the RIIA, 1987). For self-criticism see Shevardnadze's remarks at a Foreign Ministry conference in *Pravda*, 26 July 1988 – 'Perestroika, the 19th Party conference and Foreign Policy', *International Affairs* (Moscow), 1988, no. 7, pp. 3–18; V. Zhurkin, S. Karaganov, A. Kortunov, *Kommunist*, 1988, no. 1, pp. 42–50; S. Sestanovich, 'Gorbachev's Foreign Policy: A Diplomacy of Decline', *Problems of Communism*, vol. 37, no. 1 (1988), p. 3; V. Zhurkin, *Moscow News*, 1988, no. 10.

6 'Perestroika, the 19th Party Conference and Foreign Policy', *International Affairs* (Moscow), 1988, no. 7, pp. 6–7.

7 Sestanovich, 'Gorbachev's Foreign Policy'.

8 Soviet authors themselves make frequent references to Trilateral Commission publications, the Brandt Report, the Palme Commission Report, United Nations resolutions, etc.

9 Falin, *Izvestiya*, 14 March 1988; A. Yakovlev, *MEMO*, 1985, no. 3, pp. 13–15; Hough, 'Soviet Perspectives on European Security', pp. 36–7.

10 Shevardnadze in *Pravda*, 31 July 1985.

11 For the main elements of the 'new thinking' see Gorbachev, *Perestroika*, pt. 2; 'Political Report to the 27th Congress'; Gorbachev, *Izvestiya*, 3 November 1987; Primakov, *Pravda*, 12 July 1987; E. Primakov, V. Kobysh, *Literaturnaya gazeta*, 5 July 1986; Shevardnadze's speech at the United Nations, *Soviet News*, 15 June 1988; M. Light, 'Foreign Policy', in M. McCauley (ed.), *The Soviet Union under Gorbachev* (London, Macmillan, 1987), pp. 210–30; A. Pravda, *Soviet Foreign Policy Priorities under Gorbachev* (London: Routledge for the RIIA, forthcoming).

12 *Summary of World Broadcasts*, 4 September 1985. On the USA, see Bovin in *Izvestiya*, 16 November 1983.

13 In the words of one of the leading Soviet theorists of international relations: 'So long as the bipolar balance of forces is preserved at the global level, along with everything that goes with it: the system of military alliances and allied obligations, the dependence of the West European states and Japan on the USA's military power . . ., so long will the corresponding role of the states in question be preserved.' A. Pozdnyakov, *MEMO*, 1987, no. 10, p. 40.

14 Baranovsky, *Politicheskaya integratsiya v Zapadnoi Evrope*, p. 213; first quotation from Knyazhinsky (ed.), *Zapadnoevropeiskaya integratsiya*, p. 147.

15 *Izvestiya*, 4 October 1985.

16 V. Zagladin on Soviet Television, 'Studio Nine', 6 February 1988, *Summary of World Broadcasts*, SU/0069, p. A1/5 (8 February 1988).

17 'Perestroika, the 19th Party Conference and Foreign Policy', *International Affairs* (Moscow), 1988, no. 10, pp. 10, 37.

18 'Perestroika, the 19th Party Conference and Foreign Policy', pp. 36–7. In view of the context in which it was made, this remark can probably be taken at face value.

19 A. Bovin, *Izvestiya*, 25 September 1985; A. Karelov, *International Affairs* (Moscow), 1985, no. 11, p. 25.

20 Adomeit, 'Capitalist Contradictions and Soviet Policy', p. 5. See also Pridham, 'The Soviet View of Current Disagreements', pp. 17–18.

21 H. Adomeit, 'Gorbachev's Policy toward the West: Smiles and Iron Teeth', *Soviet Foreign Policy* (Proceedings of the Academy of Political Science, vol. 36, no. 4, New York, NY, 1987), pp. 98–100.

22 J. Haslam, 'Soviets take fresh look at Western Europe', *Bulletin of the Atomic Scientists*, 1988, May, pp. 38–42.

23 *Pravda*, 17 May 1988.

24 Kovalev, under the pseudonym Vtorov, and Karelov, *International Affairs* (Moscow), 1986, no. 6, pp. 97–9; Falin, *Pravda*, 16 September 1986. Other statements by and information about Kovalev and Falin are cited in Chapters 1 (note 16) and 3 (note 45).

25 See the editorial article by V.M. Berezhkov, *SShA*, 1986, no. 2, pp. 3–13; A.A. Kokoshin (a deputy director of the USA Institute), *SShA*, 1985, no. 2, pp. 3–14.

26 One ex-employee of the Soviet Foreign Ministry reports Gromyko as saying, 'We have Dobrynin in Moscow. What else can the Americans want?' A.N. Shevchenko, *Breaking with Moscow* (New York, NY, A. Knopf, 1985), p. 196.

27 Zhurkin, *Moscow News*, 1988, no. 10, p. 7. See Primakov's positive account of American policy in *Literaturnaya gazeta*, 5 February 1986.

28 *Soviet News*, 25 January 1989. Arbatov and Primakov both share a broadly 'Atlanticist' perspective. It is noticeable that Zagladin, whose statements sometimes have a 'strong Europeanist' colouring, chooses to stress the *continuity* of Soviet policy. In February 1988 he said that if the USSR had at any time 'underestimated' Western Europe, this had long since been overcome: 'The turning point for this was the 27th CPSU Congress, which announced the European direction as one of the main ones.' Soviet Television, 'Studio Nine', 6 February 1988, *Summary of World Broadcasts*, SU/0069, p. A1/3 (8 February 1988).

29 *Soviet News*, 23 July 1986. Cf. Gorbachev's comment to Genscher: 'Disrupting the existing political and territorial set-up in Europe would lead only to chaos and a worsening of the situation.' *Soviet News*, 23 July 1986. On Soviet isolation and loss of control of events,

see A. Lynch, *The Soviet Study of International Relations* (Cambridge, Cambridge UP, 1987), p. 64.

30 See R. Legvold's comments about the Soviet focus on 'contextual security'. 'The Soviet Union and Western Europe', in W.E. Griffiths (ed.), *The Soviet Empire: Expansion and Detente* (Lexington, MA, Lexington Books, 1976), pp. 244–5; M. MccGwire, 'A Mutual Security Regime for Europe?', *International Affairs* (London), vol. 64, no. 3 (1988), p. 376.

31 Pridham, 'The Soviet View', p. 25; L. Freedman, 'The United States Factor', in E. Moreton, G. Segal (eds.), *Soviet Strategy Toward Western Europe* (London, Allen and Unwin, 1984), p. 87; Z. Brzezinski, 'The Future of Yalta', *Foreign Affairs*, Winter 1984/85, pp. 279–302. A different view is put by Legvold, 'The Soviet Union and Western Europe', p. 238.

32 Legvold, 'The Soviet Union and Western Europe', p. 228.

33 Yu. Karelov, *International Affairs* (Moscow), 1985, no. 11, pp. 25, 28; Borko, *MEMO*, 1988, no. 2, pp. 32–50. In this sense, Soviet policy can be described as 'West European', 'pan-European', *and* 'Euro-Atlantic', in Adomeit's terms. H. Adomeit, 'Gorbachev's Policy toward the West: Smiles and Iron Teeth', p. 94.

34 The new favourable tone in reporting of EC affairs in the mass-circulation press is well demonstrated, for example, in the article by G. Dadyants reprinted from *Sotsialisticheskaya industriya* in *Moscow News*, 1988, no. 10, supplement.

35 Presnyakov, Iordanskaya, *MEMO*, 1987, no. 11, p. 82.

36 A. Bykov, *International Affairs* (Moscow), 1986, no. 1, pp. 92–3.

37 Gorsky at the round-table discussion, *MEMO*, 1987, no. 5, p. 103; see, too, Iordanskaya's contribution; also Chapter 3, above. 'Missing the boat' is Dadyants' expression. *Moscow News*, 1988, no. 10, supplement.

38 A. Bykov, *Moscow News*, 1988, no. 2, p. 3; *The Financial Times*, 18 December 1987; *Christian Science Monitor*, 20/26 August 1987; I. Artem'ev, F. Halliday, *International Economic Security: Soviet and British Approaches* (London, RIIA Discussion Papers, no. 7, 1988), pp. 36–7.

39 A. Stent, 'The USSR and Western Europe', *The Washington Quarterly*, vol. 5, no. 4 (1982), pp. 93–5; Hassner, 'Europe between The United States and the Soviet Union', esp. p. 23; K. Dawisha, 'Soviet Ideology and Western Europe', in E. Moreton, G. Segal (eds.), *Soviet Strategy Toward Western Europe* (London, Allen and Unwin, 1984), p. 34; R. Legvold, 'The Soviet Union and Western Europe', p. 234.

40 Kniazhinsky, *West European Integration*, pp. 358–75; Knyazhinsky

(ed.), *Zapadnoevropeiskaya integratsiya*, pp. 129, 132; Baranovsky, *Politicheskaya integratsiya v Zapadnoi Evrope*, pp. 243–4.

41 For example in Willy de Clercq's address to the European Parliament in June 1988, reported in the *Christian Science Monitor*, 20/26 June 1988.

42 *Le Monde*, 15/16 November 1987; *The Financial Times*, 2/3 July 1988.

43 K. Dawisha, *Eastern Europe, Gorbachev and Reform* (Cambridge, Cambridge UP, 1988), p. 206.

44 Asmus, 'The Dialectics of Detente and Discord', pp. 743–74; Dawisha, *Eastern Europe, Gorbachev and Reform*, pp. 160–2; G. Wettig, 'The Soviet View', in E. Moreton (ed.), *Germany between East and West* (Cambridge, Cambridge UP for the RIIA, 1987), pp. 43–5; A. Rahr, 'Gorbachev's Personal Staff', *Radio Liberty Research Report* 216/88, 30 May 1988; A. Brown, 'How Much Change in the USSR?', *World Policy Journal*, Winter 1986–7, pp. 72–4.

45 *Izvestiya*, 3 November 1987. On the general question of the relationship of bloc cohesion to internal viability of the East European regimes, see J.F. Brown, 'Soviet Interests and Policies in Eastern Europe', in R.D. Vine (ed.), *Soviet-East European Relations as a Problem for the West* (London, Croom Helm, 1987), pp. 56–67; E. Moreton, 'Foreign Policy Perspectives in Eastern Europe', in K. Dawisha, P. Hanson (eds.), *Soviet-East European Dilemmas* (London, Heinemann for the RIIA, 1981), pp. 172–94.

46 Adomeit, 'Capitalist Contradictions ', p. 16. The case is put at greater length in his book *The Soviet Union and Western Europe: Perceptions, Policies, Problems* (Kingston, Ontario, Queen's University, 1979), p. 165. Cf. W.E. Griffith, 'The Soviets and Western Europe: An Overview', in Ellison (ed.), *Soviet Policy Towards Western Europe*, p. 17; A. Ulam, 'Europe in Soviet Eyes', *Problems of Communism*, vol. 32, no. 3 (1983), p. 27; B. Racine, 'La France et les FNI', *Politique étrangère*, 1988, no. 1, p. 81.

47 For instance by Aleksandr Bovin and Deputy Foreign Minister Aleksandr Bessmertnykh in May and June 1987 respectively; by Vitaly Zhurkin in March 1988. *The Guardian*, 21 November 1987; *Moscow News*, 1988, no. 10.

48 O. Obichkin in the discussion in *International Affairs* (Moscow), 1988, no. 7, p. 13.

49 N. Portugalov, *Moscow News*, 1988, no. 9, p. 6; Gorbachev in talks with Lothar Späth, *Pravda*, 10 February 1988.

50 Afanasevsky, Tarasinkevich, Shvedov, *International Affairs* (Moscow), 1988, no. 5, p. 29 (in English).

51 See R. Laird's description of Moscow's 'anticoalitional strategy'. 'The Soviet Union and the Western Alliance', *Proceedings of the Academy*

of Political Science, vol. 36, no. 4 (New York, NY, Academy of
Political Science, 1987), pp. 106–17.

52 See Shevardnadze's statement, *Pravda*, 26 July 1988.

53 E. Moreton, 'The German Question in the 1980s', in Moreton (ed.),
Germany between East and West, p. 4.

54 A. Yakovlev, *SShA*, 1985, no. 7, p. 15. A seminar on revanchism was
organized in Prague in September 1984, Gromyko issued a public
warning about it in November and WTO Foreign Ministers did so
again in December. L. Bezymensky, *International Affairs* (Moscow),
1985, no. 3, pp. 30, 38; Asmus, 'The Dialectics of Detente and Discord', pp. 754–7; K. Dawisha, *Eastern Europe, Gorbachev and Reform*,
(Cambridge, Cambridge UP, 1988), p. 116; G. Wettig, 'The Soviet
View', in Moreton (ed.), *Germany between East and West*, pp. 43–4.

55 G. Wettig, 'The Soviet View', p. 45; Rakhmaninov, *International
Affairs* (Moscow), 1988, no. 4, p. 53; *Pravda*, 17 July 1988; TASS
Release, 13 October 1987, *Summary of World Broadcasts*, SU/8700, p.
A1/9 (16 October 1987). The Soviet side of the SPD-CPSU joint
committee included Dobrynin, Zagladin and Primakov.

56 For instance H.-D. Genscher in *Report from the Federal Republic of
Germany*, 4 January 1988; in *The Guardian*, 21 January 1988. See, too,
D. Marsh, *The Financial Times*, 15 February 1988.

57 See Yu. Krasin's analysis of SPD literature in *MEMO*, 1988, no. 4, p.
26; *The Financial Times*, 15 February 1988.

58 E. Kautsky refers to ideas floated in Bonn by Valentin Falin in
autumn 1987 for withdrawing foreign troops and allowing closer
relations between the two halves of Germany; also to rumours that
the USSR had formed a working group (Falin, Arbatov, Portugalov,
Mel'nikov) to consider the future of Germany. 'Are Soviet Attitudes
Towards Bonn Changing?', *Radio Free Europe Background Report*,
no. 194, 22 October 1987.

59 See Shevardnadze's statement in Bonn on 18 January 1988: 'Let
history solve what cannot be.' *Soviet News*, 20 January 1988. Also
Gorbachev's unequivocal comments to von Weizsäcker and Genscher
in July 1987 (*Soviet News*, 15 July 1987); and to Kohl in Moscow in
October 1988 (*Pravda*, 25 October 1988); Gorbachev, *Perestroika*,
pp. 199–201. A whole string of spokesmen have used virtually identical language to put over the same message. See E. Grigor'ev (deputy
editor of *Pravda*) on Soviet Television, 'Rezonans', 7 April 1988,
Summary of World Broadcasts, SU/0127, p. A1/7 (16 April 1988),
Aleksandr Bovin in *Izvestiya*, 18 June 1987. The statements made by
Falin and others were swiftly disavowed by Soviet and East German
officials. *Summary of World Broadcasts*, SU/8700, p. A1/11 (16
October 1987); SU/8707, p. A1/10 (24 October 1987).

60 Grigor'ev on Soviet Television, 'Rezonans', 7 April 1988, *Summary of World Broadcasts*, SU/0127, p. A1/7 (16 April 1988).
61 'Europe in Soviet Eyes', p. 30. Cf. Adomeit, *The Soviet Union and Western Europe*, pp. 55, 161; E. Moreton, G. Segal, 'Introduction', in Moreton, Segal (eds.), *Soviet Strategy Toward Western Europe*, p. 8; Griffiths, 'The Soviets and Western Europe', p. 8. Some writers were more cautious about the future of Soviet policy: K. Dawisha, 'Soviet Ideology and Western Europe', in Moreton, Segal (eds.), *Soviet Strategy Toward Western Europe*, p. 37; K. Pridham, 'The Soviet View of Current Disagreements between the United States and Western Europe', *International Affairs* (London), vol. 59, no. 1 (1983), pp. 27–8; Hough, 'Soviet Perspectives on European Security'.
62 Adomeit, 'Capitalist Contradictions', p. 7. Summarized by him from Christoph Royen, *Die sowjetische Koexistenzpolitik gegenüber Westeuropa: Voraussetzungen, Ziele, Dilemmata* (Baden-Baden, Stiftung Wissenschaft und Politik, Nomos, 1978).

Chapter 6

1 J. Hough, *Soviet Leadership in Transition* (Washington, DC, Brookings Institution, 1980), pp. 109–30; J. Snyder, 'The Gorbachev Revolution', pp. 109–12; M. MccGwire, 'A Mutual Security Regime for Europe?', *International Affairs* (London), vol. 64, no. 3 (1988), pp. 370–4.
2 Pozdnyakov, *MEMO*, 1988, no. 5, p. 13. Although endorsed at the top level, Pozdnyakov's view is questioned by Second Secretary of the CPSU Ligachev (*The Guardian*, 15 August 1988) and by other theorists. G. Wettig, '"New Thinking" on Security and East-West Relations', *Problems of Communism*, vol. 37, no. 2 (1988), pp. 1–14.
3 H. Adomeit, 'The Impact of Perestroika on Europe', paper delivered at the Royal Institute of International Affairs, December 1988, p. 17; *Pravda*. 24 November 1981; *Pravda*, 19 December 1984. For a sustained example of the specialist approach mentioned, see Yu.P. Davydov, *SShA*, 1985, no. 8, pp. 44–55.
4 Hassner, 'Europe between the United States and the Soviet Union', p. 23.
5 V. Lomeiko, *Moscow News*, 1988, no. 39. Compare G. Vorontsov in *MEMO*, 1988, no. 9, p. 44: 'It would be paradoxical to deny the presence of close linguistic, historical, cultural, political, military and other ties between the Old and New World.'
6 Vorontsov, *MEMO*, 1988, no. 9, p. 43; Yu. Borko, V. Orlov, *MEMO*, 1988, no. 9, p. 47.
7 Shevardnadze, cited in *Soviet News*, 28 January 1989.
8 V.F. Petrovsky on Soviet Television, 'Studio Nine', 6 February 1988,

Summary of World Broadcasts, SU/0069, p. A1/4 (8 February 1988); M. Maksimova, *MEMO*, 1988, no. 10, p. 64. Compare Shevardnadze's speech to the CSCE on 19 January 1989: 'The formula of community, now in the making from the Atlantic to the Urals, is marked by the shining spirit of Europeanism.' *Soviet News*, 25 January 1989.

9 The idea that Europe might serve as a test-bed for inter-system economic cooperation is current in the West as well. See, for example, Pinder, 'Integration in Western and Eastern Europe', p. 134.

10 V. Sobell, 'The Small Economic Significance of the EEC-CMEA Accord', *Radio Free Europe Research Report*, RAD BR/92 (27 May 1988); Artemiev, Halliday, *International Economic Security*, pp. 41–67.

11 The last phrase was used by Geoffrey Howe at the NATO Council meeting in Madrid, 9 June 1988. *The Guardian*, 10 June 1988.

12 TASS release, 12 September 1988, on Shevardnadze's talks with the Austrian Foreign Minister Alois Mock, *Summary of World Broadcasts*, SU/0265, p. A1/1 (24 September 1988); Vranitzky on Austrian Television, 11 October 1988, *Summary of World Broadcasts*, SU/0285, p. A1/5 (18 October 1988).

13 *Soviet News*, 12 October 1988.

14 V. Zagladin on Soviet Television, 'Studio Nine', 6 February 1988, *Summary of World Broadcasts*, SU/0069, p. A1/4 (8 February 1988). There were still warnings about German revanchism appearing in the Soviet press in 1988. Yudanov, *MEMO*, 1988, no. 9, p. 92; V. Mikhailov, *Pravda*, 24 April 1988.

15 *Eastern Europe, Gorbachev and Reform*, pp. 196–205, 211, 213. See also P. Windsor, 'Stability and Instability in Eastern Europe and their Implications for Western Policy', in Dawisha, Hanson (eds.), *Soviet-East European Dilemmas*, p. 211; Freedman, 'Managing Alliances', *Foreign Policy*, no. 71 (1988), p. 80.

16 P. Williams, 'West European Security and American Troop Withdrawals', *Political Quarterly*, vol. 59, no. 3 (1988), p. 372; L. Freedman, 'Managing Alliances', pp. 66, 80–3, 85.

17 For an eloquent expression of West European anxieties, see P. Lellouche, 'L'après-Washington', *Politique étrangère*, 1988, no. 1, pp. 153–67.

SOVIET JOURNAL
ARTICLES CITED

N. Afanasyevsky, E. Tarasinkevich, A. Shvedov, 'Between Yesterday and Today', *International Affairs* (Moscow), 1988, no. 5, pp. 22–33.

V. Amirov, B. Bolotin, O. Ivanova, Yu. Krasheninnikov, 'Tekushchie problemy mirovoi politiki', *MEMO*, 1986, no. 10, pp. 65–84.

V. Avakov, F. Kamov, S. Sokol'sky, 'Tekushchie problemy mirovoi politiki', *MEMO*, 1988, no. 7, pp. 65–84.

A. Beletsky, 'What Lies Behind the European Defence Initiative Project?', *International Affairs* (Moscow), 1986, no. 6, pp. 49–55.

V.M. Berezhkov, 'Velikaya nauka – zhit' vmeste', *SShA*, 1986, no. 2, pp. 3–13.

L. Bezymensky, 'The Wild Dreams of Modern Revanchists', *International Affairs* (Moscow), 1985, no. 3, pp. 29–37.

Yu. Borko, 'Ambitions and Realities of a "United Europe"', *International Affairs* (Moscow), 1985, no. 2, pp. 143–5.

Yu. Borko, 'O nekotorykh aspektakh izucheniya protsessov zapadnoevropeiskoi integratsii', *MEMO*, 1988, no. 2, pp. 35–50.

Yu. Borko, B. Orlov, 'Razmyshleniya o sud'bakh Evropy', *MEMO*, 1988, no. 9, pp. 46–58.

A. Borodaevsky, 'Internationalisation and Economic Integration in the Capitalist World', *Social Sciences*, 1985, no. 2, pp. 81–93.

A. Bovin, 'Western Europe: "Strategic Concerns"', *International Affairs* (Moscow), 1985, no. 12. pp. 94–103.

A. Bovin, V. Lukin, 'Na poroge novogo veka', *MEMO*, 1987, no. 12, pp. 50–62.

M. Bunkina, N. Petrov, 'Vsemirnoe khozyaistvo – ekonomicheskii fundament mirnogo sosushchestvovaniya', *MEMO*, 1986, no. 9, pp. 49–57.

A. Bykov, 'New Stage of STR and East-West Economic Ties', *International Affairs* (Moscow), 1986, no. 1, pp. 87–95.

A. Bykov, 'Two Europes or One?', *Moscow News*, 1988, no. 2, p. 3.

A. Bykova, N. Shmelev, 'Konkurentsiya i kooperatsiya na mirovykh rynkakh "vysokoi tekhnologii"', *MEMO*, 1986, no. 9, pp. 58–69.

G. Dadyants, 'CMEA and EEC – Moving Towards Each Other', *Moscow News*, 1988, no. 10, supplement.

Yu.P. Davydov, 'Soedinennye Shtaty i obshcheevropeiskii protsess', *SShA*, 1985, no. 8, pp. 44–55.

Yu.P. Davydov, 'SShA-Zapadnaya Evropa: bremya partnerstva', *SShA*, 1987, no. 5, pp. 3–14.

V. Falin, 'Po povodu novykh "istoricheskikh debatov"', *MEMO*, 1987, no. 12, pp. 73–84.

A. Grigoryants, 'Europe – Our Common Home', *International Affairs* (Moscow), 1986, no. 4, pp. 81–89.

S.A. Karaganov, 'Zapadnaya Evropa, SShA i problemy razoruzheniya', *SShA*, 1987, no. 10, pp. 25–34.

S.A. Karaganov, 'Europe: Looking to the Future', *Moscow News*, 1988, no. 34, p. 3.

Yu. Karelov, 'USSR-Western Europe: Guidelines of Cooperation', *International Affairs* (Moscow), 1985, no. 11, pp. 23–8, 75.

E. Kirichenko, 'On Certain Specific Features of Inter-Imperialist Rivalry', *International Affairs* (Moscow), 1985, no. 6, pp. 78–86, 106.

G. Kirillov, 'The Moscow Treaty: A Basis for USSR-FRG Relations', *International Affairs* (Moscow), 1985, no. 9, pp. 29–35.

V. Kobysh, E. Primakov, 'U poroga tret'ei tysyacheletiya', *Literaturnaya gazeta*, 5 February 1986.

A.A. Kokoshin, 'Diskussii po tsentral'nym voprosam voennoi politiki SShA', *SShA*, 1985, no. 2, pp. 3–14.

T. Kosyreva, 'Perspektivy regional'nogo ekonomicheskogo sotrudnichestva', *MEMO*, 1988, no. 1, pp. 143–5.

Yu. Krasin, 'Novoe myshlenie vo vzaimootnosheniyakh kommunistov i sotsial-demokratov', *MEMO*, 1988, no. 4, pp. 23–33.

V. Kremenyuk, 'Zapadnaya Evropa: integratsiya v sfere vneshnei politiki', *MEMO*, 1987, no. 10, pp. 142–3.

A. Kudryavtsev, 'Istoki, real'nosti, perspektivy "tekhnologicheskoi Evropy"', *MEMO*, 1986, no. 10, pp. 26–40.

V. Lavrenov, 'O nekotorykh aspektakh vozmozhnogo rasshireniya EES', *MEMO*, 1978, no. 6, pp. 53–63.

N. Lebedev, 'Soviet Efforts to Ensure European Security', *International Affairs* (Moscow), 1985, no. 8, pp. 3–12.

V. Lomeiko, 'Reflections on a Common European Home', *International Affairs* (Moscow), 1987, no. 12, pp. 103–12.

S. Madzoevsky, S. Skladkevich, 'Zapadnoevropeiskii tsentr: tendentsii v razvitii voennykh vzaimosvyazei', *MEMO*, 1978, no. 1, pp. 91–100.

M. Maksimova, 'Kapitalisticheskaya integratsiya i mirovoe razvitie', *MEMO*, 1978, no. 3, pp. 12–23; no. 4, pp. 14–24.

M. Maksimova, 'Raskryt' potentsial sotrudnichestva', *MEMO*, 1988, no. 10, pp. 61–8.

D. Mel'nikov, 'Zapadnoevropeiskii tsentr: aspekt politicheskii', *MEMO*, 1978, no. 5, pp. 19–29.

V. Mil'shtein, 'Genezis neoglobalizma', *MEMO*, 1988, no. 1, pp. 148–9.

I. Osadchaya, 'Smena strategii regulirovaniya v kapitalisticheskikh stranakh', *MEMO*, 1987, no. 10, pp. 13–28.

V. Pan'kov, 'Sotsial-demokraty ob ekonomicheskom sotrudnichestve v Evrope', *MEMO*, 1987, no. 10, pp. 121–7.

T. Parkhalina, 'NATO – za fasadom "atlanticheskogo edinstva"', *MEMO*, 1986, no. 7, pp. 104–10.

Ya. Pevzner, 'Novye podkhody k analizu mezhdunarodnykh ekonomicheskikh svyazei kapitalizma', *MEMO*, 1986, no. 10, pp. 97–102.

E. Pletnev, 'Za politiko-ekonomicheskii podkhod k kategorii vsemirnogo khozyaistva', *MEMO*, 1985, no. 7, pp. 106–13.

I. Ponomareva, N. Smirnova, 'SShA – Zapadnaya Evropa: rozn' ekonomicheskikh interesov', *MEMO*, 1986, no. 8, pp. 131–6.

N. Portugalov, 'Warsaw Treaty Superiority?', *Moscow News*, 1988, no. 9, p. 6.

E. Pozdnyakov, 'Vzaimosvyaz' ekonomiki i politiki v mezhgosudarstven-nykh otnosheniyakh', *MEMO*, 1987, no. 10, pp. 28–41.

E. Pozdnyakov, 'Natsional'nye, gosudarstvennye i klassovye interesy v mezhdunarodnykh otnosheniyakh', *MEMO*, 1988, no. 5, pp. 3–17.

E. Primakov, 'Novaya filosofiya vneshnei politiki', *Pravda*, 10 July 1987.

V. Razmerov, Yu. Fedorov, 'Dve tendentsii v mezhimperialisticheskikh otnosheniyakh', *MEMO*, 1988, no. 1, pp. 3–19.

G. Rozanov, 'USSR-FRG Ties and International Relations in Europe', *International Affairs* (Moscow), 1985, no. 1, pp. 133–5.

Yu. Rubinsky, 'Zapadnoevropeiskaya integratsiya na novom etape: institutsional'nyi aspekt', *MEMO*, 1987, no. 12, pp. 85–90.

Yu. Rubinsky, 'European Community: "Political Dimensions"', *International Affairs* (Moscow), 1988, no. 2, pp. 41–9.

A. Shapiro, 'Eshche raz k voprosu o teorii vsemirnogo khozyaistva', *MEMO*, 1985, no. 3, pp. 91–102.

A. Shapiro, 'Protivorechiya mezhdunarodnogo gosudarstvenno-monopolisticheskogo regulirovaniya ekonomiki', *SShA*, 1985, no. 3, pp. 27–39.

Yu. Shiryaev, 'The World Economy in the Context of the Technological Revolution', *Social Sciences*, 1986, no. 1, pp. 72–84.

Yu. Shishkov, 'The EEC in a Vicious Circle of Problems', *International Affairs* (Moscow), 1985, no. 10, pp. 64–73.

Yu. Shishkov, 'Evropeiskoe soobshchestvo na perelomnom etape', *MEMO*, 1986, no. 6, pp. 40–53.

Yu. Shishkov, 'Interimperialist Rivalry Escalates', *International Affairs* (Moscow), 1986, no. 5, pp. 28–36.

N. Shishlin, 'Prokladyvaetsya doroga v zavtra', *MEMO*, 1988, no. 8, pp. 5–9.

N. Shmelev, 'Interstate Regulation of the World Capitalist Economy: New Tendencies', *International Affairs* (Moscow), 1985, no. 9, pp. 61–9.

Yu. Stolyarov, E. Khesin, 'Sovremennyi kapitalizm i neravnomernost' razvitiya', *MEMO*, 1987, no. 5, pp. 17–31.

V. Stupishin, 'Indeed, Nothing in Europe is Simple', *International Affairs* (Moscow), 1988, no. 5, pp. 69–73.

I. Tyulin, 'A Book on French Foreign Policy', *International Affairs* (Moscow), 1984, no. 4, pp. 136–7.

L. Vidyasova, 'Western European Integration as Part of the Aggressive Plans of Washington', *International Affairs* (Moscow), 1985, no. 6, pp. 107–16.

S. Volodin, 'Britain and Peace in Europe', *International Affairs* (Moscow), 1982, no. 3, pp. 31–40.

G. Vorontsov, 'SShA – Zapadnaya Evropa: obshchnost' i protivorechiya na novom etape', *SShA*, 1984, no. 4, pp. 3–13.

G. Vorontsov, 'Ot Khel'sinki k "obshcheevropeiskomu domu"', *MEMO*, 1988, no. 9, pp. 35–45.

A. Vtorov, 'USSR-France: Towards Understanding and Detente', *International Affairs* (Moscow), 1985, no. 12, pp. 3–8.

A. Vtorov, Yu. Karelov, 'The Dynamic European Policy of the USSR', *International Affairs* (Moscow), 1986, no. 6, pp. 96–106.

S. Vybornov, A. Gusenkov, V. Leontiev, 'Nothing is Simple in Europe', *International Affairs* (Moscow), 1988, no. 3, pp. 34–41.

A. Yakovlev, 'Imperializm: sopernichestvo i protivorechiya. Voprosy teorii', *Pravda*, 23 March 1984.

A. Yakovlev, 'Istoki ugrozy i obshchestvennoe mnenie', *MEMO*, 1985, no. 3, pp. 3–17.

A. Yakovlev, 'Opasnaya os' amerikano-zapadnogermanskogo militarizma', *SShA*, 1985, no. 7, pp. 3–15.

A. Yakovlev, 'Mezhimperialisticheskie protivorechiya – sovremennyi kontekst', *Kommunist*, 1986, no. 17, pp. 3–17.

Yu. Yudanov, '"Evrika" – problemy sozdaniya zapadnoevropeiskogo tekhnologicheskogo obshchestva', *MEMO*, 1986, no. 9, pp. 93–100.

Yu. Yudanov, 'FRG vo vtoroi polovine 80-kh godov – osnovnye problemy i poiski ikh resheniya', *MEMO*, 1988, no. 9, pp. 82–93.

V. Zhurkin, 'Unique Future of Europe', *Moscow News*, 1988, no. 10, p. 7.

V. Zhurkin, 'Vstrecha v Vashingtone', *SShA*, 1988, no. 1, pp. 5–10.

V. Zhurkin, S. Karaganov, A. Kortunov, 'Vyzovy bezopasnosti – starye i novye', *Kommunist*, 1988, no. 1, pp. 42–50.

R.I. Zimenkov, A.B. Parkansky, 'Popytka ottesnit' konkurentov', *SShA*, 1985, no. 10, pp. 15–25.

Round-table discussions and conferences

'Gosudarstvennoe regulirovanie i chastnoe predprinimatel'stvo v kapitalisticheskikh stranakh: evolyutsiya vzaimootnoshenii', *MEMO*, 1987, no. 3, pp. 56–68.

'Perestroika, the 19th Party Conference and Foreign Policy', *International Affairs* (Moscow), 1988, no. 7, pp. 3–18.

'Sovremennoe sostoyanie i itogi razvitiya zapadnoevropeiskoi integratsii', *MEMO*, 1987, no. 5, pp. 94–103.

'Strany Zapadnoi Evropy v programmakh SOI i "Evrika"', *MEMO*, 1988, no. 2, pp. 129–35.

'Vneshnyaya politika i diplomatiya', *Pravda*, 26 July 1988.

Related titles

The Soviet Union and India
Peter J. S. Duncan

India is the only non-communist country in the Third World with which the Soviet Union has managed to maintain friendly relations over a prolonged period. Has this friendship persisted because of Soviet influence on India, Indian influence on the Soviet Union, or a coincidence of geostrategic interests? This paper examines the costs and benefits to the Soviet Union of its substantial economic and military involvement with India, and assesses how India fits into Soviet policies towards southwest Asia and China. The author analyses the effects on Soviet-Indian relations of the invasion of Afghanistan and of the military build-up in Pakistan; how changing domestic and global priorities in Moscow and New Delhi will affect the relationship; and what the role of the West should be.

The Soviet Union and Syria
Efraim Karsh

This paper examines the nature of Soviet relations with Syria, assessing the commitments made and the gains reaped by Moscow and Damascus in the economic, military and political spheres. After discussing Soviet interests in the region generally and in Syria in particular, the author traces the evolution of the relations between the USSR and its main Middle Eastern ally since Asad came to power in 1970. Whilst arguing that huge military aid has intensified the pro-Soviet alignment of Syrian policy, the study contends that Asad's perception of his country's national interests has also played a large part in shaping the relationship. The author concludes that both sides have gained from what is an interdependent relationship.

The Nuclear Predicament:
Explorations in Soviet Ideology
Stephen Shenfield

Ideological debate is one component of the intellectual background to Soviet policy-making. This paper explores how Soviet writers wrestle with the challenge to their ideology that is posed by the threat of nuclear war. What, for example, is the relationship between the values of peace and of socialism? What drives the arms race? Is capitalism inherently militaristic, or is a demilitarized capitalism conceivable? Is the outcome of history predetermined or open? It is shown that the range of permissible views is wider than often assumed, and that the constraints of Soviet ideology do not exclude evolution towards a more cooperative approach to international security.

ROUTLEDGE